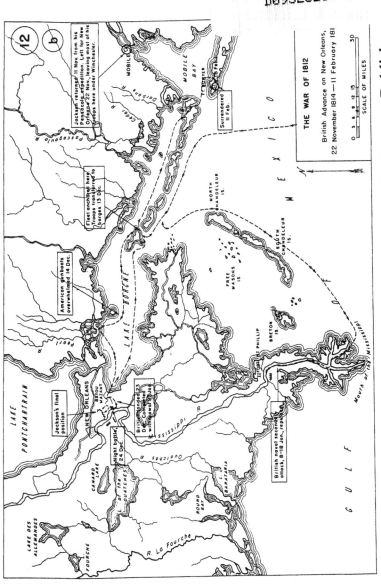

Map 12B, Esposito, West Point Atlas of American Wars 2V, Praeger Publishers.
Permission for use from Greenwood Publishing Group, Inc., Westport, Ct.

Oil on canvas of General Andrew Jackson in military uniform by his dear friend Ralph E. W. Earl. Painting is proudly displayed in and reproduced by permission of the Hermitage: Home of President Andrew Jackson

CHALMETTE

THE BATTLE FOR NEW ORLEANS
AND HOW THE BRITISH
NEARLY STOLE THE LOUISIANA TERRITORY

by CHARLES PATTON

HICKORY TALES PUBLISHING
Bowling Green, Kentucky
April 2001

Library of Congress Card Catalog Number 2001087282

ISBN 0-9709104-0-1

First edition April 2001

Additional copies may be obtained from:

HICKORY TALES PUBLISHING
841 Newberry St.
Bowling Green, Kentucky 42103

To Sylvia & Shelley

Forward

It has been my pleasure over the last three years to read and study all the literature that I could find relating to the remarkable *Battle of New Orleans*. It had been my intention to take the most powerful passages of these books and weave them into a powerful narrative of the British assault. The master historian of this arena is, of course, Robert V. Remini. Other prominent authors were Robin Reilly (a British viewpoint) and Frank L. Owsley. A reading of the bibliography at the end of this book will give anyone, who is interested, a list of some of the available books to read concerning the *Battle of New Orleans*.

I would like to thank the *North Carolina Inter-Library Loan* system. This feature of our local library allowed an author in a rural setting to have access to research material that otherwise would not have been available.

CONTENTS

*"...they who are in possession of the Mississippi River,
will in time command that continent."*
- Dupratz's History of Louisiana, London 1774

Chalmette

Chapter One

A Maritime Rival

In 1865, at the close of the American Civil War, if you had asked any American older than sixty years of age when they despaired most for their republic's very existence. They would have quickly answered that it was fifty years previously, during the first thirty-seven days of 1815 when they were all but certain that America would be conquered and split asunder.

In fact, that was the plan. In the spring of 1814 the War Office in London was confidently laying out detailed plans for a knockout blow to the United States of America. This calculated blow was designed to fracture the United States into two or three different nations and wrest New

Orleans and the Louisiana Territory away from them. From the final battle of the American Revolution at Yorktown to the present day, America has never been closer to destruction.

Americans tend to think that the Battle at New Orleans was needlessly fought. Few people realize what was at stake at the *Battle of New Orleans* and what the British Lion really had in mind with the assault on New Orleans. An American victory on January 8th, 1815 was absolutely crucial for it's survival and future.

Prior to the Civil War the people of the United States knew the importance of the victory at New Orleans and celebrated it with parades every year, but with the tremendous impact of the Civil War fifty years later it's importance has been all but forgotten.

The causes of the War of 1812 had its roots in the ending of the American Revolution and to a small part the purchase of the Louisiana Territory. After the revolution a succession of British Prime Ministers never gave up their hope of regaining their lost colonies in America.

John Adams, while serving as the first American minister to England after the American Revolution, wrote back to the American Secretary of Foreign Affairs, "The popular pulse seems to beat high against America. The people are deceived by numberless falsehoods...so that...if this nation had another hundred million to spend, they would soon force the ministry into a war against us...Their present system, as far as I can penetrate it, is to maintain a determined peace with all Europe, in order that they may war singly against America."[1] "Britain has ventured to begin commercial hostilities. I call them hostilities, because their direct object is not so much the increase of their own wealth, ships, or sailors, as the...[reduction]...of ours. A jealousy of our naval power is the true motive, the real passion which actuates them; they consider the United States as their rival, and the most dangerous rival they have in the world."[2] "If they can bind Holland in their shackles, and France, by her internal distractions, is unable to interfere, she [Great Britain] will make war immediately against us."[3]

England was so contemptuous of the United States that they would not even send an ambassador to America as the United States had done with John Adams to England. In 1788 Adams was recalled in protest and the position went unfilled until 1792.

In 1805 while Monroe was minister to England he "...felt that the attitude of Great Britain towards the United States at this time was...designed to subject American

Commerce to every restraint in its power. He attributed the attitude of Great Britain to her great jealousy of the increasing prosperity of the United States and to her determination to leave nothing untried which would tend to impair that prosperity."[4]

Great Britain, unable to free themselves from the shackles of European war and entanglements, continued to be locked into a fierce war in Europe. For twenty-one years, from 1793 to 1814 Britain and much of Europe fought for their very survival. The drain in men and money was enormous. The cost of survival against France called for ruthless measures. This meant imposing heavy taxes upon itself and it's colonies to finance the war. It also meant it had to have every available man for its army and navy.

This led to conflict with America. England's shortage of sailors became so serious that they started impressing American seaman, many of who were former British subjects and sailors. They felt that once an Englishman, always an Englishman. Contempt for Americans ran rampant throughout the British mindset. This attitude of disrespect and contempt for America was based on the belief in American cowardice.

The purchase of the Louisiana Territory also agitated the English toward the Americans. At the time, Napoleon had secretly negotiated the *Treaty of Amiens* with the Spanish, which ceded the Louisiana Territory to France. President Jefferson on hearing these rumors knew that this could be a serious problem because Napoleon had boasted of controlling shipping on the Mississippi by occupying New Orleans. Jefferson wrote, *"There is on the globe one single spot,...the possessor of which is our...habitual enemy. It is New Orleans, through which the produce of three-eighths of our territory must pass to market... The day that France takes possession of New Orleans...we must marry ourselves to the British fleet and nation."*[5] To keep from having an alliance with England, whom he despised, he sent ambassadors to France to try to buy New Orleans and possibly Florida.

Soon after the ambassadors arrived in Paris and made their desires known, Napoleon came to a surprise decision. He called in Marbois, head of the French Treasury and Berthier, Minister of War, to instruct them to sell the whole Louisiana Territory to the Americans. Berthier and Marbois were stunned. Two hundred years of struggle and French settlement, done away with on a whim.

Napoleon explained that he had an idea while taking a bath. Since France had lost the war in Haiti, including some 20,000 men, he could not hope to establish a French Colonial Empire in the Western Hemisphere. France's withdrawal would cause a vacuum, which he knew the English were only too eager to fill. Therefore, to keep the English from taking control he would sell the land to the Americans and finance the upcoming war with England at the same time.

Marbois very politely asked Napoleon if he was sure he knew what he was doing. Napoleon replied, *"I am fully [aware] of the value of Louisiana. I do not under valuate Louisiana...I regret parting with it, but I am convinced that it would be folly to persist in trying to keep it...I have scarcely received it before I am run the risk of losing it; but if I am obliged to give it up, it shall hereafter cost more to those [England] who force me to part with it, than those to whom I yield it [United States]. The English have successfully taken from France: Canada, Cape Breton, Newfoundland, Nova Scotia, and the riches portions of Asia. They are engaged in exciting troubles in St. Domingo. They shall not have the Mississippi, which they covet... They have twenty vessels in the Gulf of Mexico, and our affairs ...are daily getting worse...The*

conquest of Louisiana might be easily made [by England],
and I have not a moment to lose in putting it out of their
reach...I am inclined, in order to deprive them of all
prospects of ever possessing it, to cede it to the United
States...They only ask for one city of Louisiana [New
Orleans], but I consider the whole country lost, and I
believe that in the hands of this rising power it will be more
useful to the...interests of France, than if I should attempt
to retain it."[6] This..."strengthens forever the power of the
United States; and I have just given to England a maritime
rival that will, sooner or later, humble her pride."[7]

The loss of the colonies in the American Revolution combined with their growth of territory with the Louisiana Purchase greatly disturbed Great Britain but "the greatest single cause of war was [American] nationalism, and it was nurtured by a lofty condescension, amounting at times to open contempt, explicit in British dealings with the American ex-colonists. The tacit refusal of the British to regard the Americans as anything more than immature and disaffected colonials was as much responsible for war as were the untiring efforts of the [American] Hawks who promoted it."[8] "By 1812 the [animosity] between United States and Britain...[started]...by the Revolution had become a national tradition.".[9]

To put it simply, "Europe really disliked the United States.... The problem centered on European fear and envy. Because the United States was a free nation based on a broad suffrage that tolerated an expanding democracy, there was considerable resentment abroad. Democracy represented a danger to the crowned heads of Europe. If the American "experiment" succeeded, it would serve as a guide... to the rest of the radical factions in Europe".[10] Many in Europe hoped for the failure of the American experiment.

By 1812 the British were beginning to hurt from President Madison's embargo against Britain. They needed every commercial advantage in their war with France and Napoleon. They decided to relent in their persecution of the United States by rescinding the Orders in Council that forbade American ships to dock anywhere in Europe unless it was a British port. At the same time on the other side of the Atlantic, the American War Hawks finally got their way. President Madison and Congress declared War on Britain.

When this declaration of war reached England the British were infuriated. They felt that they were carrying on a righteous war against the despotic dictator, Napoleon, and that they, alone, were carrying the torch for freedom. They felt that they had been "stabbed in the back" by their American cousins. For the moment their hands were tied with Napoleon, but they would not forget this insult and they would strike back when the chance came and get back what was rightfully theirs.

England could only afford to send a few punitive raids against America for the first couple of years, but they were successful in almost everything they did. The United States would only appoint as generals people who served in the Revolutionary War. This meant that all the generals were over sixty years old. Their efforts had no energy or daring. From 1812 until the fall of 1814, the English troops struck and roamed at will with hardly any effective resistance from the Americans.

Chapter Two

Oh, Muscogees! Brethren of my mother!

During the French and Indian War, the American Revolution, and now the War of 1812, the English had done a good job of keeping up cordial relations with the Indians. One of the effects of this was the power and influence of the Indian Chief, Tecumseh. At the beginning of the war Tecumseh, along with his brother the Prophet, toured the southern states of Tennessee, Alabama and Georgia to visit with the Creek Indians. Tecumseh wanted to form a confederacy of tribes to drive the white man from their lands.

At the time the American policy toward the Indians was one of assimilation. This was starting to work well in some areas and was spreading. There were many Indians living life like and as white men. Farming was beginning to take hold among the Creeks. Tecumseh and his brother meet with tribe after tribe trying to counter this trend.

Tecumseh's brother, the Prophet, preached his way of life like an extremist religion. All ways of the white men were bad, it was wrong to farm; the only acceptable way was to do it like they had always done, which was to hunt and fish.

At the annual Creek council Tecumseh made a speech before 5,000 people. "He told the gathering that he had come from the Great Lakes of the North and had passed through the settlements of the whites "like the wind at night. No war-hoop was sounded, no track was made, no fire was kindled," but, he said, "there is blood on our war clubs"..."They have made women of our warriors and harlots of our women". Then Tecumseh raised his voice, *"Oh, Muscogees! Brethren of my mother! Brush from your eyelids the sleep of slavery, and strike for vengeance and your country. The red men have fallen as the leaves now fall. I hear their voices in those aged pines. Their tears drop from the weeping skies. Their bones bleach on the hills of Georgia. Will no son of those brave men strike the pale face and quiet these complaining ghosts? Let the white race perish! They seize your land; they corrupt your women; they trample on the bones of your dead! Back whence they came, upon a trail of blood, they must be driven! Back—aye, back in the great water whose accursed waves brought them to our shores! Burn their dwellings-*

destroy their stock-slay their wives and children, that the very breed may perish. War now! War always! War on the living! War on the dead! Dig their very corpses from their graves. The redman's land must give no shelter to a white man's bones".[11]

"The Shawnee warrior promised that arms would be sent from across the sea. In the North they would be received at Detroit and in the South at Pensacola. He told the Creeks that he would leave his prophets with them to stand by their sides and "catch the bullets of their enemies". [12]

Before Tecumseh began his southern tour the British had told him of the approach of a comet that would come soon. Also there had been much earthquake activity about that time. He told his Creek brothers to watch the skies and feel the earth because when they see his arm of fire in the sky it would be a signal that he was on the warpath and he would stamp his foot and the earth would shake. As foretold the comet came and an earthquake destroyed much of an important Creek Indian village. He gained many believers with these signs.

For the next couple of years there was much controversy among the various Creek tribes. Many of them wanted to go on the warpath with Tecumseh but some were more careful and feared the United States government. The younger generations were for war but the older ones feared it. Feelings came to a fevered pitch when Creek tribes and families who opposed the war on the whites were murdered by the warring faction of the Creeks. A virtual civil war broke out within the Creek nation.

This hostility among themselves continued until the Prophets took full control and organized a raiding party that attacked Fort Mills in Alabama. The fort was completely defeated. Reports show that 247 men, women and children were killed. Some of the Prophets were so enthralled with their own belief in magic that they cast aside their white man's gun and fought with magic, war clubs, and bows and arrows. Women were scalped, and those who were pregnant were opened while alive and their embryo infants put on the ground, young children were taken by the legs and had their brains beaten out against the fort walls. When their chief, Weatherford, saw what was going on, he tried to stop the barbarity, but the warriors were so enraged that they threatened to kill him, and he had to back off for his own safety.

When word reached the rest of the southern states about the massacre a great outcry came for revenge. In Tennessee, Governor Blount appointed Andrew Jackson to head a punitive expedition to destroy the Creek nation. This was Andrew Jackson's chance to get into the war. He had offered his services to President Madison and Congress many times but had always been rebuffed. His reputation as duelist and a hothead while serving in Congress led many leaders to believe that he was too volatile and they wanted no part of him. Thomas Jefferson had called him "the most dangerous man in America", but this time he was appointed by the Governor of Tennessee and not Congress.

This was the second time that Governor Blount had commissioned Jackson for a war effort. The first time was in 1812 when there was a perceived English threat at New Orleans. Jackson had marched his men to Louisiana and had been there a short time when his army was promptly disbanded near New Orleans by orders from Washington. Jackson was furious. Most of his army were young men from the age of eighteen to twenty-two and this was their first time away from home. They were sons of families he knew back in Tennessee and he knew almost every soldier by name. He realized that if he disbanded in Louisiana that many of the young men would have trouble making it back to Tennessee along the notorious Natchez Trace without coming to harm. He refused to disband and started the march back to Nashville, supplying and feeding the army at

Andrew Jackson

Young Andrew Jackson, from around the time of the Battle of New Orleans. Portrait by Charles Phillips from a painting by Jarvis, taken from live sitting 1815. Permission for use obtained from the Hermitage: Home of President Andrew Jackson.

his own expense. There were 150 men on the sicklist, of whom 56 were bedridden. He ordered his officers to turn their horses over to the sick along with his three personal horses and he constantly walked back and forth through his army making sure they were making it and that there were no stragglers.

The soldiers thought he was the toughest man they had ever seen so they nicknamed him after the one of the toughest things they knew of, a hickory tree. They affectionately called him *"Old Hickory"* and he became immensely popular when they arrived back in Tennessee and the state found out how he had cared for their young sons whom the federal government had abandoned.

In September, 1812 Lt. James Stirling of the British ship *Brazen* docked in Pensacola, Florida. Because Pensacola had been named by Tecumseh as a place to get weapons and ammunition, Indians were constantly meeting here to trade and talk with British representatives. Lt. Stirling wrote a report to the Britain's Governor Cameron of the Bahamas, which was passed on to the British War Office. This report suggested that the Gulf Coast was vulnerable to a naval supported action. He also pushed the theory that the best way to attack was with the help of the Creek nation. He stated, "They still have the highest attachment to the English, and the greatest hatred to the American name..."[13]

In December, 1813 Governor Cameron sent Lt. Edward Hanfield to assess the situation along the Gulf Coast. Lt. Hanfield landed in Pensacola and meet with two Creek leaders who happened to be there in search of arms. One of the Creeks was an Indian with the very European name of Alexander Durant. Durant sent an Indian interpreter with a letter to Governor Cameron stating his desire for a British commission. The letter stated, *"We hope you will eade and asist us as your alis and friends. Sir you know that our four fathers owned the Lan Wher we now live But and Ever since our father the King of Grate Briton Left us, the Americans has Bin Robing us of our Rights and now the americans has maid war against our nations and we aply for armes and amenisun to defend our silves from so Greid a Enemy and as you Know that this nations all ways was frinds to the English, we hope you will send us Seplys By Henry Durgen [Indian Interpreter] as soon as possible and we hope that you will send sum of our old friends, the British troops to eade and asist us a ganst our Enemeys."*[14] Governor Cameron of the Bahamas sent these military reports and letters of request to Lord Bathurst, British Secretary of State for War and Colonies.

These reports formed the basis of the planned gulf coast invasion in 1814 by Admiral Cochrane.

Even through the Creeks were promised guns and ammunition at Pensacola they rarely got it. The Spanish who officially controlled the territory were afraid to supply the Indians for fear that the Americans would retaliate. The British followed a line of giving just enough powder and lead for hunting purposes. Because of Fort Mills the Creeks now faced a full-fledged war from the Americans with only minimal guns and powder. It would take the British over a year before they would respond with the needed guns and ammunition. The Creeks had struck prematurely.

Four armies proceeded to attack the Creek nation. One from west Tennessee, one from east Tennessee, one from Georgia, and one was the U.S. Army's Third Regiment coming up from New Orleans. The only two that made any impact were Andrew Jackson's west Tennessee army and the Georgia army. The Georgia army had an initial success under General Claiborne at Holy Town. According to the Indian Prophet, Josiah Frances, Holy Town had been made sacred by the Great Spirit. He claimed that it was protected by an invisible barrier and that any white man passing through it would be killed instantly.

When General Claiborne's troops began firing on the town the prophet's men fired a few rounds back and then waited for Claiborne's troops to march into the barrier and fall dead. When this failed to happen the Creeks were badly shaken and fled. Chief Weatherford and about thirty of his men stood to the side and watched the spectacle. They were some of the few Creeks who did not believe in the prophet's magic. After the other Creeks fled they offered the only real resistance of the day. Soon Weatherford's men had to flee because of superior numbers, but Chief Weatherford stayed until it was almost too late. He was forced to make a dramatic escape by jumping off a sixty-foot ravine into the river atop his horse.

After this battle the Creeks had a few minor victories under Chief Weatherford's leadership but it would soon turn to disaster for the Creek nation. General Jackson's favorite subordinate, General Coffee, won an impressive victory at Ten Islands. This was soon followed by Jackson's win at Talladega. Since Jackson's initial victory, there were many tribes of the Creek nation who had decided that it was not a wise thing to fight against the Americans and the tribe at Talladega was one of these. Chief Weatherford had surrounded this village and had every intention of killing all within as an example to all opposing tribes. General Jackson heard of the siege and marched his men to rescue the besieged Indian town. His attack turned the tide on the village and soon he had the attacking Creeks surrounded. There were close to 1,000 braves with Weatherford and it looked like Jackson's army might kill them all, when a break occurred in Jackson's line and 700 braves escaped.

The final and decisive battle of the Creek War was the Battle of Horseshoe Bend. It ended the Creek War and almost wiped out the Creek nation. Horseshoe Bend is in central Alabama and is a piece of land in which the Talapoosa River wraps around a peninsula of land in the shape of a horseshoe. It was a gathering spot for the Indians and was well know to Jackson's army. There were over a thousand Creeks waiting for Jackson in the horseshoe.

When Jackson arrived he was dumbfounded. The Creeks, under Chief Menawa, had built a breastwork of trees across the 350-yard open end of the horseshoe. The breastwork was five to eight feet tall and had double portholes for firing. Jackson later wrote to General Pickney, "It is impossible to conceive a situation more eligible for defense than the one they had chosen...and the skill which they manifested in their breast work, was really astonishing".[15]

Jackson fired his artillery against the breastwork with almost no effect for two hours. Jackson was becoming frustrated and the Indians were dancing and howling insults at his men. Meanwhile, General Coffee sent his men to the backside of the horseshoe on the other side of the river where several friendly Indians along with some of Coffee's men swam across the river and set fire to the huts at the back of the Creek compound. Coffee's force was too small to do any real damage but it provided a diversion that Jackson immediately pounced on. Jackson ordered a charge. His men rushed the breastwork with both sides firing at point blank range through the portholes. Major Montgomery mounted the breastworks and called for his men to follow him. He was immediately shot through the head. His second in command, Ensign Sam Houston, climbed to the top of the wall and called for an advance. He was shot in the upper thigh with an arrow but he jumped into the compound and continued fighting. His men followed him. The breach was made. The fighting was savage and in many places hand to hand. The Indians gave no mercy and requested none. Though only one in three had guns they fought to the death. After a few minutes the Creeks started a retreat to the back of the compound and took devastating rounds of fire in doing so.

Jackson sent in a white flag and an interpreter to ask for their surrender but they replied with derision and a blast of gunfire that killed one member of the flag party. Jackson's men responded with artillery and devastating rifle fire. Davy Crockett wrote, "We shot them like dogs". Still they would not surrender. The Creeks hid themselves on the cliffs of the river and Jackson shot his artillery at them. This had little effect so they set fire to the brushy cliff sides. The Indians had to run but most were shot and killed. The only thing that stopped the fighting was darkness when they could no longer see their targets. The next day Jackson ordered a count of the bodies. There were 557 dead on the battle field, 300 dead in the river, and a few more found in the woods, for a total of about 900 Creeks killed. But Chief Weatherford was not among them. By chance he had been gone that day on other business. Jackson was greatly disappointed; he wanted him to pay for the attack on Fort Mills.

Jackson offered protection to all Creeks who would take his pardon and do as he commanded. Many that were left, including the chiefs, had little choice but to comply. The American army had destroyed most villages and almost all the food supplies. The only hope for their families was at the mercy of Andrew Jackson, whom the Creeks now called "Sharp Knife".

The next day Chief Weatherford boldly rode into Jackson's camp, approached Jackson and surrendered under the provisions of Jackson's pardon. Jackson was stunned and upset at the request for pardon. Chief Weatherford spoke, "I am Witherford: I am in your power. Do with me what you please, I am a soldier still. I have done the white people all the harm I could. I have fought them, and fought them bravely. If I had an army, I would fight them still. But I have none! My people are no more!! Nothing is left to me but to weep over the misfortunes of my county."[16]

A flustered Jackson spoke to Weatherford, "I had directed that you should be brought to me confined, had you appeared in this way, I would have known how to treat you".[17] Then Jackson, knowing that he had to honor the pardon request, said to him in a condescending voice, "...if you choose to try the fate of arms once more, and I take you prisoner, your life shall pay for forfeit of your crimes."

Weatherford drew himself to his full height, looked Jackson straight in the eye and spoke with deep emotion, "Well you may speak to me in this style, now. There was a time, when I had a choice. I have none, now-even hope is ended: Once I could animate my warriors; but I cannot animate the dead. Their bones are bleaching on the plains of Tallushatches, Talladega, and Emuckfau: and I have not surrendered myself without reflection. While there was the smallest hope, I remained firm at my post, nor... [asked]... for peace. But, my warriors are no more: The miseries of my nation affects me with deepest sorrow." Here he became choked with emotion and could not speak for a few moments. Then he continued, "But I desire peace for the few that are left...you are a brave people- you are a brave man; and I rely on your generosity. You talk a good talk: My people shall listen to it".[18]

Jackson was impressed, so impressed that he invited Weatherford into his tent where they talked at length. Jackson pardoned him and allowed him to keep his rifle and his lands. Weatherford stayed true to his word and lived in peace with the white man. He even visited General Jackson at the Hermitage before he died.

At Horseshoe Bend the tremendous struggle for control of North America ended and ownership changed hands, especially for the Indians east of the Mississippi. For the Indians west of the Mississippi, their only hope was with the British conquest of the Louisiana Territory and the creation of a buffer zone between the Indians and the Americans.

The Creek war made Jackson a hero in the western states but it permanently shattered his health. He started the Creek War fresh from a bullet wound he had gotten in a dual. He soon contracted dysentery. "…once he contracted dysentery he could not shake it off, and his body took a fearful beating. When attacks were particularly severe in the field he doubled over the branch of a tree; in camp he pressed his chest against the back of a chair. …For nourishment … he swallowed weak gin and water. Throughout the war he suffered many days of pure agony when he thought he would collapse because of the pain. Yet he forced himself to keep going. He would not indulge his body….By the end of the war his…[health]… was half wreaked but his will power had grown to monumental proportions".[19]

Chapter Three

The Cossacks spared Paris,
but we spared not the Capital of America

In Washington, President Madison was deeply troubled. Nothing had gone right since the beginning of the war and the treasury was almost penniless. But he and the administration were beginning to see that they had a general that could wins battles in the south. Now they did not care if he was volatile or not politically correct, he could win battles. He moved Jackson out of the Tennessee militia and promoted him to a three star general in the regular army.

In Europe, Napoleon had finally been defeated. England had fought against the European continent for thirty years and now they alone were left standing. Their military machine had been brought to a peak with all necessary military equipment and veteran troops. They could be compared to the United States when the Soviet

Union imploded in the early1990's. They, alone, were left standing as a superpower and no one could stand against them.

Now Lord Bathurst and the War Office were turning their attention toward America. Their plan was to conquer the northern United States by coming down Lake Champlain, a second force would raid up and down the East Coast to draw American troops toward the large coastal cities. Then sweep around to the Gulf Coast, land their forces at Mobile, and march westward just above New Orleans which would effectively cut it off, leaving the city no choice but to surrender. They would then advance up the Mississippi River and meet with British troops coming out of Canada. This would effectively box in the United States. All coastal cities would be blockaded, the gulf would be under British guard, the Mississippi would be held by British troops and small ships, and finally Canada would close the lid on the box.

When Admiral Cochrane first proposed this plan he only asked for 3,000 men. He felt he would have added support of the Creek Indians, Spanish and freed American slaves as Governor Warren had suggested back in 1812. But the War Office became so enamored with the plan they eventually committed 12,000 men to the effort. They were to come from Britain, France, Canada, Italy and South Africa. It was one of the largest expeditionary forces they had ever launched with the sole purpose of taking away from the United States the territory gained from the Louisiana Purchase.

The War Office was so confident of victory that when they consulted the Duke of Wellington, Britain's greatest military mind, they brushed aside his reservations. Wellington felt that there was no one place to capture that would cause the Americans to surrender. He remembered well the American Revolution when the Americans lost almost every battle except the last one. They did not fight like Europeans, who surrendered after they lost a few battles. These people just melted into the woods after a loss and came back again and again until they had worn the enemy down and then they would finally pounce on a weak spot for a victory. He thought that it would turn to a type of guerilla warfare with no clear objectives. When consulted by the navy he tried to tell Admiral Cochrane that there were not any suitable landing places or supply lanes near New Orleans but he was brushed aside. At this point he became suspicious that the military leaders in charge were more interested in military plunder than military values. When Wellington was later asked about leading the expedition he begged off, stating that he was needed in Europe in case military concerns again rose there.

In the summer of 1814 when the British started their campaign against the East Coast Jackson's army was sent to Mobile to protect against a possible British invasion.

In Ghent, Belgium, the British and American ambassadors were finally meeting in an effort to resolve the war. The British first demanded that the United States cede much of the New England states, areas north of central Ohio and New Orleans as terms for peace. Astounded, the American diplomats flatly refused.

The British press started at this time to sway British opinion against the United States. The London *Times* stated that Mr. Madison was a liar and an imposter, ..."Mr. Madison's dirty, swindling manoeuvres in respect to Louisiana and the Floridas remain to be punished...With Madison and his perjured set no treaty can be made, no oath can bind them....Our demands can be couched in a single word,-Submission."[20]

In London, an American gentleman went into a prominent map makers shop inquiring about maps of North America. The proprietor, not recognizing him as an American stated confidentially to him that he should, "...defer the purchase for a few weeks; that he was then keeping all his maps unfinished, as the boundaries would all be changed, and a considerable part of the Union [would be] incorporated with the British possessions!"[21]

By summer 1814 Admiral Cochrane's east coast invasion of America was in full swing under the command of Admiral Cockburn and General Ross. British troops landed on the Chesapeake Bay near Washington. They swept through the few militia troops at nearby Bladenburg and came straight into the city of Washington unopposed. Admiral Cockburn and General Ross were some of the first troops to ride into Washington. For the second time that day General Ross's horse was shot out from under him by a sniper. They immediately began the systematic burning of the capital. Captain Harry Smith of the British 95th Regiment wrote in his journal, "We entered Washington for the barbarous purpose of destroying the city. Admiral Cockburn would have burnt the whole, but Ross would only consent to the burning of public buildings. I had no objection to burn[ing] arsenals, dockyards, frigate buildings, stores, barrack, etc., but well do I recollect that, fresh from the Duke [of Wellington's] humane warfare in the South of France, we were horrified at the order to burn the elegant Houses of Parliament and the President's house..."[22] Ross and Cockburn personally directed the destruction of the White House, the Capitol, the main bridge over the Potomac, the Treasury, the War Office, the National Archives, the offices of Washington's leading newspaper the *National Intelligencer*, barracks, stores, and powder magazines.[23] Captain Smith was chosen to take a ship back to England to report of Washington's destruction. Smith was taken in before the Prince Regent who was ruling during the illness of King George III. The prince looked intently at the map that showed which government buildings were burned. Captain Smith later wrote, "In his heart I fancied I saw [that] he thought it a barbarian act."[24]

The London *Times*, at that time a mouthpiece for the British government, gloried over the destruction of the public buildings in Washington saying, "That ill-organized association is on the eve of dissolution, and the world is speedily to be delivered of the mischievous example of the existence of a government founded on democratic rebellion." The London *Statesman* saw it differently by stating... "Willing would we throw a veil of oblivion over our transactions at Washington. The Cossacks spared Paris, but we spared not the capital of America."[25]

Cockburn took personal mementos from both the Congress and the President's House. While all the destruction was taking place General Ross spent much of

BRITTON 01

his time making sure personal property and civilian life was safe. He even posted guards to safeguard certain residences and buildings. He had two soldiers whipped for looting and had a third shot. Admiral Cockburn rode among the citizens asking mockingly, "Where is Jimmy"?, meaning President James Madison. The British government wanted very much to capture both President Madison and his wife Dolley to parade around in England. Later in life when Admiral Cockburn had his portrait painted he used a burning Washington, D.C. as a background.

During the afternoon of their second day in Washington a ferocious thunderstorm or possibly a hurricane hit Washington. "The ferocity of the winds humbled the British and scared seasoned locals. It came upon Washington with an advance of thunder and lightning, swirling winds, and a darkening sky. The gusts hummed and whirred as they picked up velocity until they set off a frightening roar. Electrical storms were common to the area, but it was rare for the sun to be eclipsed so early. Bolts of lightning illuminated scenes of chaos. Tumultuous winds ripped off roofs and carried away feather beds. The violent weather toppled three chimneys off the common roof of the Patent Office and General Post Office. A whirling, unseen force, it buckled the chains of the drawbridge across the Potomac… Trees were uprooted and fences downed. A few houses collapsed upon the unsuspecting enemy. Some of the older homes were lifted off their foundations and dashed to pieces. Soaked British combat troops caught in the open lay flat on the ground, fearful of making a run for it. Others broke ranks and scattered for cover. One officer on horseback rounded a corner and caught the blast head-on. In an instant both he and his horse were blown to the ground. The winds scooped up several light cannons and bore them off like paperweights, dumping them at random in the turmoil…An eyewitness, Michael Shiner, rated it 'one of the awfullest storms which raged for a long time".[26]

After the storm, British troops began to regroup around a town pump when Admiral Cockburn rode up and spotted an American lady nearby.

"Great God, Madam! Is this the kind of storm to which you are accustomed in this infernal country?", he shouted.

"No Sir, she answered, "this is a special…[act of]… Providence to drive our enemies from our city."

"Not so, Madam," he countered. "It is rather to aid your enemies in the destruction of your city."[27]

Nevertheless, he and his troops promptly got on their horses and were not seen in Washington again.

General Ross, on the other hand, took his army toward Baltimore where American resistance stiffened. Ross rode to the front to observe this new American challenge. As he approached the skirmishing, two American sharpshooters shot and killed him. This act would have far reaching consequences during the upcoming battle at New Orleans. The British immediately stormed the area of the two sharpshooters and killed them. You can find today, in Baltimore, a statue commemorating sharpshooters H.G. McComas and Daniel Wells for initiating a chain of events that would help lead to the British defeat along the Gulf Coast. The death of a beloved general and the stiffening of American defenses caused the British to turn their eyes toward Fort McHenry at North Point.

Admiral Cochrane, now in charge of the British fleet, needed to capture the North Point area so that he could capture as many small, shallow-draft boats as possible. The British War Office had failed to send over any small boats for the New Orleans campaign and Cochrane knew he would need them along the Gulf Coast. The British tried in vain to take Fort McHenry with a tremendous bombardment. This bombardment failed to make the fort surrender. Most Americans remember this battle because it produced our national anthem, written by Francis Scott Key, but the important military value was that it denied Admiral Cochrane any small boats that could operate in shallow waters.

As the British were evacuating their men an incident happened at Hampton, Virginia. Some of the troops got out of hand. The city was looted and several women were raped. This shook up both the Americans and the British. Some of the British officers were shocked and questioned if they were on a military mission or a plundering rampage.

Now Admiral Cochrane could not afford to spend any more time for diversionary operations along the east coast. He was falling behind schedule and he needed to rendezvous with other British ships and troops at Negril Bay in Jamaica. It was time to concentrate on their primary mission: The capture of the Louisiana Territory and control of the Mississippi River.

In Ghent, the British peace negotiators demanded navigation rights of the Mississippi River in exchange for the right of the Americans to dry fish on the banks of a particular Canadian shore. Some of the American ambassadors were actually considering the proposal but Henry Clay threw an absolute fit and said he would not give up the Mississippi River just for the right of a few New England fisherman to dry cod fish.

The British also asked that a buffer be established up the Mississippi River and- curve around into Canada passing through Ohio and Michigan with a two hundred mile buffer zone. No one would be allowed to live in this area, White or Indian. This would stop bloody massacres on both sides, protect the Indians from American encroachment and stop American expansion. The American Ambassadors never accepted this and the British finally gave up on this demand during the final phase of the treaty negotiations, probably feeling that they could achieve this anyway after the capture of the Louisiana Territory.

While Washington was burning, Andrew Jackson was rushing toward Mobile, Alabama. He knew that Mobile was the key to the Gulf Coast. If the British captured Mobile then they could sweep west and capture the whole southwest territory. When Jackson arrived at Fort Bowyer across the bay from Mobile he found it abandoned. Jackson immediately sent Major William Lawrence with 160 men to repair and man the fort. Within forty-eight hours of Jackson's arrival in Mobile he also learned that the British had landed an advance force under Colonel Nichols at Pensacola, Fla. They were occupying the Spanish city and were recruiting Indians for the upcoming campaign. Jackson wanted to go after the British right then but he did not have enough men.

He knew the invasion was on and he needed more men. He immediately sent word to the Governors of Tennessee and Kentucky to raise an army and send them south to him. Legend has it that he asked a Mohegan Indian, Holdfast Gaines (Sleeping Bear) to deliver the message to General Carroll in Nashville within ten days. He made the trip from Mobile to Nashville in an incredible six days through rough and unfriendly terrain.[28] It would be two months before they would begin to arrive.

The advance guard of the British also knew the value of Mobile. Sir William Percy, of the *HMS Sophie*, boasted he could take Fort Bowyer in twenty minutes. He, along with Colonel Nicholls on board, attacked Fort Bowyer on September 14, 1814.

Major Lawrence and his 160 men had pulled off a small miracle in getting the fort back on a defensible footing in such a short time. The British ships pulled up in a line and started a bombardment with their naval guns. At the same time a land force attacked from behind a bluff near the fort. A few blasts from the fort's cannons silenced the British land troops. Colonel Nichols, aboard the *HMS Hermes*, was wounded when a cannon blast blinded him in one eye with a wooden splinter. The fort and the ships fired at each other for a couple of hours with little effect until the Americans landed a lucky shot. A cannon blast from the fort severed the anchor cable of the *Hermes*. The *Hermes* drifted into easy gunfire range of the fort and was raked from stem to stern. It was soon abandoned and set afire. When she exploded General Jackson heard it thirty miles away in Mobile.

The British took stock of their situation. Colonel Nichols was wounded and the fort's cannon fire had been better than expected. They now considered Mobile too strong to take, although in reality it was not. In Jamaica Admiral Cochrane discovered that his invasion plans of New Orleans had been leaked out and there was definite proof that warnings had been sent to General Jackson's force. Cochrane now made the biggest mistake of his career. Instead of trying to retake Mobile with a proper invasion force he decided to bypass Mobile and try to beat Jackson's army to New Orleans.

Admiral Cochrane was now moving on the Gulf Coast with the full British might to take the Louisiana Territory based on three big assumptions:

First. The British were expecting to arm large numbers of Indians who would help them in their invasion, but their plans and rifles (22,000 of them) for the Creek Indians were one year too late. General Jackson had decimated the Creeks and there were hardly any warriors left to fight. What Indians were left had a healthy respect and fear of "Sharp Knife" (General Jackson).

Secondly. The British expected the Spanish to help them. But when Colonel Nichols had landed his British troops in Pensacola they had freed the slaves and acted very highhanded toward the Spanish. As a result the Spanish officials were glad to see them leave. When Jackson's re-enforced troops arrived and quickly shoved the British out, it convinced any doubtful Indians that it was not wise to fight "Sharp Knife". Jackson had quickly taken Pensacola from the Spanish and just as quickly had given it back to them. The Spanish governor having watched how dismally the British had performed, grabbed Jackson's arm and thanked him profusely saying, "God to preserve your life many years."[29] Now the British could not expect any help from the Spanish.

And *thirdly*. To attack by way of Pensacola or Mobile. Then sweep west and north of New Orleans, isolating it. This path had the added benefit of keeping the British out of the Louisiana swampland. But now Jackson had changed their mind by his stiff resistance at Mobile and Pensacola. Admiral Cochrane had now committed the army to a frontal attack on New Orleans by trying to beat Jackson's army there.

"Had...[Jackson] not conquered the Creeks, Mobile could not have been held; and if Pensacola had not been taken, the British would have used it as an invasion route into the United States, and then across to the Mississippi. The invasion would have been infinitely simplified...The invasion of Florida also vastly improved his [Jackson's] own talents in handling the army. The speed with which he could now maneuver his men was truly extraordinary.[30]

Chapter Four

Hostilities shall not be suspended

During Jackson's invasion of Pensacola and Mobile he constantly received warnings from Washington and various Caribbean sources that New Orleans was the primary intended target. Jackson had a hard time believing this because he knew that an invasion at Mobile was the best place for the British attack. Then Jackson received definite word from Washington, through the peace negotiators at Ghent, that New Orleans was the invasion point. Word also arrived that Cochrane's fleet had left Jamaica for New Orleans.

With so much advance warning about New Orleans Jackson decided to check on the city's defenses. Still thinking that Mobile was the probable invasion point, he left it heavily fortified. He sent word to General Coffee, who had now reached the northern part of Louisiana, to station himself at Baton Rouge, La. so that he could respond to either Mobile or New Orleans. Jackson with a few of his officers left Mobile and arrived in New Orleans on December 1, 1814. Jackson arrived as emaciated and sick as ever from his constant battle with dysentery. He wrote Rachel, his wife, that, "I was taken verry ill...there were eight days on the march that I never broke bread. My health is restored but I am still verry weak."[31]

In London the atmosphere of good feeling was giving way to guarded caution. On the European continent Napoleon had escaped and was coming back to France to revive his army. The United States had suddenly stiffened in its resistance against their three pronged attack. Commander McDonough had defeated the British fleet in the Battle of Lake Champlain in September, 1814. The Battle of North Point at Fort McHenry had been a stalemate with General Ross killed in the process. The British War Office quickly dispatched General Edward Packenham by fast frigate to replace General Ross. Packenham had written orders from Lord Bathurst stating, ... *"Proceed to Plymouth and embark there for Louisiana to assume command of the forces operating for the reduction of that Province".*[32] He was to catch the fleet at Jamaica and proceed with the troops to New Orleans but Admiral Cochrane's decision to beat Andrew Jackson's army to New Orleans had left

Packenham playing catch up to the fleet. It was strongly rumored that he carried in his personal dispatch case letters appointing him Governor of Louisiana and a promise of an appointment as an Earl back home in England.

The fleet was now arriving off the coast of Louisiana near New Orleans. It was practically a colonizing expedition. "Civil officers were already on board to conduct the government of Louisiana. The Honorable Mr. Elwood from Trinidad was to be lieutenant governor. A gentleman from Barbados was to be collector of the Port of New Orleans. He had with him his five, blond daughters...An attorney general, an admiralty judge and a secretary for the colony had been sent directly from England. The Superintendent of Indian Affairs had come from Canada. On board the fleet's ships, the officer's wives and other females with the expedition anticipated a gay season in New Orleans and they made life merry with music and dancing and other entertainment.[33] Letters arriving on the East Coast from England for the families with Cochrane's fleet had the forwarding address of New Orleans.

Although it was not uncommon "for a regulated number of wives to accompany their husbands on campaigns, the presence, however, of no less than 104 children embarked with one regiment (the 93rd Highlanders) is not so easily explained. Even the most liberal allowance for Scottish fecundity would leave Packenham with some 600 soldiers' children from among the ten regiments aboard the transports, an uncomfortable burden for any army but more acceptable to one [theory] which proposed to settle in the territory it conquered."[34]

A government editor and printing press were part of the retinue. The editor would print and broadcast proclamations and other announcements, which would explain English policy to the benighted inhabitants of New Orleans, and publish orders of the new government.

English peace commissioners at Ghent knew all this. They knew that the orders of the expedition were to occupy Louisiana, ascend the Mississippi River, make a junction with the 10,000 troops from Canada, and choke off what was left of the United States. They thought the invasion and occupation of Louisiana would be easily and quickly accomplished and they had to tailor the treaty to correspond with the invasion."[35]

The English peace commissioners puzzled the Americans by declaring: "We do not admit [to] Bonaparte's construction of the law of nations. We cannot accept it in relation to the subject-matter before us".[36] This statement seemed completely unrelated to the peace process and left the American peace negotiators scratching their heads, but this was referring to the fact that the British felt that Napoleon had illegally sold the Louisiana Territory to the United States. France had held the territory in a type of guardianship for Spain in accordance with the *Treaty of Amiens*. Therefore, technically, France should not have sold the territory to the United States.

The British peace ambassadors started pushing for a "*Uti Possidetis*" proposal, meaning that each side keeps whatever territory they had gained or lost in the war. The Americans adamantly refused. Now with pressure mounting in Europe and North American resistance stiffening, they tried a new tack. The British now proposed a "mutual restoration" clause. The effect of the wording "belonging to either party, taken by the other", would have been that "all territory belonging to either party, taken by the other, should be returned", "belonging" being the key word here, since Britain had already established in a previous note that they did not consider the Louisiana Territory as a legal possession of the United States. The American ambassadors, not really happy with this phrase, toyed with the wording for the next week and finally found a phrase that satisfied both parties. The mutual restoration clause of the treaty now stated, "all places, points, and *'possessions'* whatsoever", would be returned after the war. This satisfied the British since they did not believe that Louisiana was a legal possession of the United States. The American ambassadors, only partially understanding the trap laid out for them, could only hope for the best.

The British peace commissioners had one last demand. Fearing that President Madison might not sign the treaty, they demanded that the cease fire be effective only after both governments had ratified the treaty. They counted on having a strong presence on the East Coast and a victory at New Orleans. They were very confident that they could make a separate treaty with the New England states if Madison refused to sign.[37]

This last demand, in effect, delayed the end of hostilities until mid-February. This ploy also gave the English troops as much time as possible to invade, capture, and establish control of Louisiana and the Mississippi River.

On the same day that General Jackson arrived in New Orleans, Lord Castlereagh, of the British government, not knowing that the expeditionary force was behind schedule, stated to a Paris newspaper, "I expect at this moment that most of the large seaport towns of America are laid in ashes; that we are in possession of New Orleans, and have command of all the rivers of the Mississippi valley and the Lakes, and that the Americans are now little better than prisoners in their own country."[38]

Lord Bathurst wrote to General Packenham in his instructions for the reduction of the Louisiana territory that, *"It has occurred to me that one case may arise affecting your situation upon the Coasts of America...You may possibly hear whilst engaged in active operations that the preliminaries of peace between His Majesty and the United States have been signed in Europe...As the Treaty would not be binding until it shall have received such Ratification..., it is advisable that **Hostilities should not be suspended** until you shall have official information that the President has actually ratified the Treaty; and a Person will be duly authorized to apprise you of this Event."[39]* Also, *"with the help of the [Creek Indians]...we may expect to rescue the whole province of Louisiana from the United States."[40]*

The British fleet arrived off New Orleans in early December. They spent the next couple of weeks trying to decide on an avenue of approach to New Orleans. They really wanted to attack by Lake Pontchartrain but the water was too shallow for their boats. The failure of the British

Major General E. M. Packenham who bravely died
leading his men Lithograph from a portrait in possession
of Thomas Berkeley, Esq. Published 1815. Reprinted by
courtesy of the Director, National Army Museum, London

The Battle of Lake Bourgne. Grounded American vessels await attack by the overwhelming British forces. Courtesy of the Historic New Orleans Collection. Museum/Research Center Accession number 1974.25.5.40

War Office to send any shallow-draft boats as requested by Admiral Cochrane and the failure to capture any from the Baltimore area during the Battle at Fort McHenry now made maneuvering near New Orleans almost impossible. They could not come up the Mississippi River either. Just before the city of New Orleans there was a sharp turn in the river and the fleet would have to wait under the guns of Fort St. Leon until the wind changed. The land between them and New Orleans was nothing but swamp. The most logical place to land was near Fort Coquilles and approach along a low ridge in the swamp called the Chef Menteur Road. This was the avenue that General Jackson and most of New Orleans felt would be the avenue of attack but the British felt that this avenue was too near Fort Coquilles. Cochrane had intelligence that Fort Coquilles had forty cannons and five hundred troops. This was not true but ever since Fort Bowyers at Mobile they had developed a healthy respect for American artillery skills and he was not going to put his fleet near the guns at Fort Coquilles.

Admiral Cochrane's staff did not know where to attack until two of his officers, in scouting boats, found a small Spanish fishing village. The fishermen, who were doing well selling fish to the fleet, showed them a bayou that landed them just twelve miles south of New Orleans and more importantly, dry land between the landing spot and the city.

But it was not all good news. The British fleet could not enter Lake Borgne because of it's shallowness. This meant that with the few barges they had, they would have to row thirty miles from the fleet's anchorage near Cat Island to Pea Island which was to be used as a staging point. Then they would have to row twenty miles to the mouth of the Bayou Mazant and then another ten miles up the bayou to their jump off point. This would put a huge burden on the small barges and rowing sailors. It was a very long and thin supply line for a war campaign. Months earlier in London, the Duke of Wellington, when discussing the invasion of New Orleans, pointed out the difficulty of attacking directly at New Orleans by asking the question, "Where's the navigation?" Meaning, how are you going to get there?

The British had to take care of one small detail before they could begin the invasion. They had to clear Lake Borgne of the American Navy which consisted of five small gunboats, each carrying a twenty-four pounder and two carronades.

The British sent twelve of their forty barges against the small American Navy. The Americans fully expected the attack and had planned to fall back under Fort Coquilles' heavy guns for protection, but Lake Borgne was having some extremely low tides and the wind was against their retreat to the fort. They had no choice but to form a battle line and fight. The battle was easily won by the British with both sides experiencing fairly high casualties.

This defeat on Lake Borgne was a severe blow to Andrew Jackson's intelligence system. Without the gunboats on the lake he had no way of knowing what the British fleet was up to. Now the British were free to start their assault through Bayou Mazant.

When Jackson heard of the defeat on the lake he was finally convinced that New Orleans was the real target and not a feint. He quickly dispatched messages to all his generals to come as quickly as possible. To General Coffee in Baton Rouge, La, he wrote, "You must not sleep until you reach me or arrive within striking distance." To General Carroll he wrote, "[you are]…to proceed day and night"[41] [until you reach New Orleans]. General Coffee replied to Jackson that many of his men were on foraging expeditions but he would be there in four days. He made it in three with about half his army. The rest showed up within a day or two with the sick and other supplies.

General Carroll had left Nashville with three thousand young recruits. He had been instructed by the Governor and Jackson not to come by way of the Mississippi River but he took it upon himself to do so anyway. This decision turned out to be a godsend for him. The war had made weapons a scarcity west of the Appalachian Mountains. More than half of his soldiers did not have guns or ammunition. They soon overtook a flatboat loaded with muskets and powder headed for the defense of New Orleans. They took command of the vessel and Carroll drilled his men in the use of their weapons while on the flatboats. Tennessee blacksmiths also made up 50,000 cartridges. Each cartridge included one musket ball and three buckshot. This combination of musket ball and buckshot would turn out to be deadly for the British when they would close within less than a hundred yards of the American lines. General Carroll and his men arrived in New Orleans on December 20, only two days after General Coffee's arrival.

In New Orleans Jackson had resisted the help of that "hellish banditi", Jean Laffite and his men, but they met one day on a street corner and came to terms. Laffite and his skilled artillery pirates became indispensable with their marksmanship in artillery. Laffite also became a

trusted military advisor for the rest of the campaign. Too much cannot be made of Laffite's contribution of gunpowder, cannon balls, flints and skilled artillery men in the outcome of the New Orleans campaign.

Jackson was desperate for men. Not only did he accept pirates he gladly accepted free men of color. Louisiana's Governor Claiborne had suggested that a couple of black regiments could be raised if Jackson wanted them. Jackson replied enthusiastically, writing to Claiborne saying, *"Our Country...wants Soldiers to fight her battles. The free men of colour in your city are inured to the Southern climate and would make excellent Soldiers. They will not remain quiet spectators of the interesting contest. They must be for, or against us-distrust them, and you make them your enemies, place confidence in them, and you engage them by every dear and honorable tie to the interest of the country who extends to them equal rights and privileges with white men."*[42] When the assistant district paymaster questioned the General's authority to enlist blacks in the service, Old Hickory blasted him. *"Be pleased to keep to yourself your opinions upon the policy of making payments of the troops ...without inquiring whether the troops are white, black or tea."*[43]

Chapter Five

Fair-Buck Range

On the morning of December 22, 1814, British soldiers under General Keane and Colonel Thornton set out with an advance guard of eighteen hundred soldiers. The soldiers were stacked in the small barges like cordwood standing on end. They would have to make the thirty mile trip, in barges rowed by sailors, with hardly any room to shift positions. While making this trip, Lieutenant Gleig, who wrote one of the few narratives of this campaign, stated that he did not know what real rain was until this trip. Pellet stinging, bone chilling, torrential Louisiana rain soaked everyone on the barges.

Once this campaign hit land it stopped being a navy led operation and turned into an army led campaign. General Keane had only recently been appointed a General, and it was understood that as soon as General Packenham arrived he would be the commanding general. While waiting on Packenham the British were soon to miss the experience of their fallen General Ross. Colonel Thornton had led the British at the Battle of Bladensburg near Washington and was just recovering from a wound suffered there. Keane was a newly appointed general and cautious, Thornton was battle tested and intuitive. Had Colonel Thornton been in charge of this expedition there would probably be no United States today as we now know it.

Late in the morning of December 23, Colonel Thornton and his men broke out of the swamp and onto the land of Major Gabriel Villeré. They rushed toward the plantation and the main house. Major Villeré was sitting on the porch, smoking a cigar, and talking to his brother Célestin when he saw flashes of red coming through the orange grove. He rushed through the house to escape by a back door where he was met by Colonel Thornton and several of his men and was immediately put under house arrest. Villeré had been put in charge of guarding this section of the bayous and he knew that he had to sound the alarm to General Jackson. Villeré decided on a desperate escape plan. He suddenly jumped out of his chair and flew through a window, knocking down several British soldiers in the process. He took off on a dead run for the swamp with soldiers firing at him. Thornton cried, "Catch him or kill him!" Villeré hurdled a fence and disappeared into the swamp. Thornton's men fanned out in the swamp to encircle and recapture him.

Thirty-seven years later, old and emaciated by a long sickness, and surrounded by his sons and daughters, Villeré retold the story to his children. His voice shaking and full of emotion, he told how his "recapture ... seemed inevitable, when it occurred to him to climb a large live-oak [tree], and conceal himself in its thick evergreen branches. As he was about to...[climb the tree]... his attention was attracted by a low whine or cry at his feet. He looked down and...[saw that]...his favorite setter [was] crouched piteously on the ground... The faithful...[dog]...had followed her master in his flight. What could [he] do with the poor animal? Her presence near the tree would inevitably betray him. There was no other hope of escape...With a deep sigh and eyes full of tears, ...[Villeré] seized a large stick, and struck the poor, faithful dog as she cowered at his feet, soon...[killing]...her. Concealing the dead body, he ascended the tree where he remained until the British had returned to their camp, and the pursuit was relinquished."[44]

Lt. Gleig wrote of Villeré's escape, *"One man contrived to effect his escape, ...How many a gallant life hung upon the*

54

chances of that one man's capture! How many a wife, mother, sweetheart...[would have] been spared the desolation of their lives had one of the shower of bullets, amid which he fled, have stopped his flight!" [45]

At 1:30 pm that afternoon Villeré reached Jackson's headquarters. Jackson had already heard a couple of rumors of British troops landing near Villeré's plantation but now Major Villeré gave him reliable confirmation of the landing. Jackson who had been lying down because of his sickness, slowly got off the couch, drew himself up to his full height and struck his fist on the table, exclaiming, "By the Eternal, they shall not sleep on our soil!" Then turning to his aides he said, "Gentleman, the British are below, we must fight them tonight."[46] Jackson had the alarm cannon sounded, messengers were sent to recall the city guard, the Mississippi Cavalry, the free black battalions, and Coffee's Cavalry. General Carroll and the Louisiana Militia were left to guard the Chef Menteur road in case Keane's men were a feint and the real attack was still coming by that direction.

Back on Villeré's plantation General Keane had arrived with the rest of the advance guard. Colonel Thornton was desperately trying to convince General Keane that they should march into the city of New Orleans immediately since there was no sign of American defense. Had General Keane followed Colonel Thornton's advice they would have certainly taken New Orleans but Keane recently had two intelligence reports that said that General Jackson had twenty thousand men there. He hesitated, he had several thousand more troops who would be here by the next morning and he felt much more comfortable with those additional troops than with his eighteen hundred army advance guard. He held off on the attack. General Ross's death at Baltimore now began to come into play in the form of a less experienced general. While the British troops started making camp and lighting campfires, Colonel Thornton stood alone, looking toward New Orleans, trying hard not to show his frustration. Jackson only had two thousand men at this point in time, and they were spread out all over the New Orleans area.

The word of the British arrival just a few miles from New Orleans struck terror in the hearts of the people of New Orleans. Word had reached them about the British rapes at Hampton, Virginia and the women were scared. To their credit they armed themselves with daggers and refused to flee the city even thought they were not sure about the military worthiness of the Tennessee troops. They just did not look military. The Tennesseans wore long, full coats that made them look like Quakers. On their heads they wore slouching wool hats. Some them wore raccoon or foxskin caps. They wore untanned deerskin belts with hunting knives and tomahawks stuck in them and they took extra care of their prized long rifles. Their encampment looked more like a camp meeting than a military unit. They had no military bearing or speech. One Louisianan said they only knew how to do one thing and that was to take a bead on something with their long rifle and bring it down. Every last one of them could knock a squirrel out of the tallest tree. It was a point of honor among them not to shoot a deer unless it was running. It just wasn't sporting.

Although the people of New Orleans had their doubts about Coffee's men, Jackson did not. John Coffee was Jackson's best friend. He had earned that respect and friendship by always being there when Jackson needed him. Whether it was the Creek War or now against the British, Jackson knew he could rely on Coffee and his men to accomplish whatever was asked of them, no matter how trying or distasteful. Coffee and his men were now battle hardened veterans of a brutal Indian War and a semi-war with the Spanish along the Gulf Coast. They could live off the land without grumbling. They may not have looked like a military unit but General Andrew Jackson had no doubt about their discipline or effectiveness.

From about 1:30 pm to 3:00 pm Jackson and his staff laid out a plan for their night attack. At three o'clock that afternoon Jackson mounted his horse and rode out to watch his troops pass by on their way to meet the British. Most of the New Orleans regiments paraded by, first came the black regiments, then the Mississippi Dragoons followed by Coffee's Cavalry and finally came a small regiment of Choctaw Indians under Captain Jugeat. Then Jackson looked up and exclaimed, "Ah, Here come the brave Creoles."[47] Major Planché's New Orleans battalion had run all the way from Fort St. John to reach the intended battle. Even today in New Orleans there is a race held each year starting at Fort St. John and ending near Jackson's statue in Jackson Square to commemorate this six-mile run.

The day was December 23rd, just two days since the shortest day of the year. By 5:00 o'clock it was getting dusk and the British were setting up camp and lighting their campfires. They were just eight miles south of New Orleans. They were not worried about the Americans who had never attacked at night. The Americans, in fact, had not attacked them at all on this expedition. So far they had done little but run in almost every battle. They had defended themselves well on a couple of occasions but never attacked.

As General Jackson mounted his horse and turned to join his troops, many women and children gathered around him crying and voicing their fears. He attempted to calm them by telling them to fear not, "he was there and ... the British would never get into the city, so long as he held the command."[48] Jackson had waited for this moment his whole life. It was time to pay the British back for the insults and deaths they had inflicted on his family as a teenager during the American Revolution. Vincent Nolte, a New Orleans cotton merchant, who was enlisted in one of the New Orleans regiments stated, "The General was burning with impatience to come to close quarters with the red coats...He wanted to fight. There *was* no computation of relative force..."[49]

General Coffee waited for the signal to begin the assault. They had closed within 500 yards of the British, Indian style, without being detected. Coffee and his men had been waiting for this. They had long blamed much of the Indian conflict on the British. Coffee had written to his wife, "My boys have got so used to killing Indians that they are almost sorry for them. But they have no pity for the redcoats, who, they declare, are to be held responsible for all the devilment the Indians have done. Every one of my boys wants to be within fair buck-range of a redcoat!"[50] These back woodsmen stood ready in their woolen brown, camouflage like, clothing and fox skin caps. They had their long rifles in hand and tomahawks in their belts ready for hand-to-hand combat.

At seven o'clock the gun ship *Carolina* slipped down the river in the dark. As she drew even with the British troops she cut loose with her cannon fire. Sheer panic and confusion reigned in the British camp. Cannon fire mowed down men and campfires. For ten minutes men did not know where to run or what to do, but the ever dependable Colonel Thornton finally gained control of his men and had them lie against the river levee bank which sheltered them from the cannon fire. About twenty minutes later the *Carolina* let up on her cannon fire and Andrew Jackson gave the order for the frontal attack. Jackson's men gained ground in the initial charge, but the British were veterans and under Thornton's leadership formed a good defensive line. Then General Coffee's men swung in from the left side and again it looked bleak for the British as hand-to hand combat ensued.

Lt. Gleig wrote of the fierce night battle, *"In the whole course of my military career, I remember no scene at all resembling this. We fought with the savage ferocity of bull-dogs, and many a blade, which till to-night had not drank blood, became in a few minutes crimsoned enough*".[51] Just then, right in the middle of the battle, several hundred reinforcements arrived in barges from Bayou Mazant. They were the British 21st Royal Fusiliers and the 93rd Scottish Highlanders. Lt. Gleig again wrote, *"There cannot be a doubt that we should have fallen to a man had not the arrival of fresh troops at this critical juncture turned the tide of affairs."*[52]

At this point fog rolled over the battlefield and things became confused. British fired at British, Americans fired at Americans. Men were captured, rescued, and recaptured. After conferring with General Coffee, Jackson ordered a retreat to the Rodriquez Canal.

Later that night, following the battle Lieutenant Gleig went in search of his best friend. As he searched over the battlefield, "the most shocking and most disgusting spectacles, everywhere met...[his]... eyes," men with "wounds more disfiguring, or more horrible " than he had ever witnessed; men shot through the head or heart, or stabbed to death from bayonets, hunting knives, or sabers; men dead from heavy blows to the head from the butt ends of muskets...the faces of the dead "exhibited the most savage and ghastly expressions." In several places he saw an English and American soldier with "the bayonet of each fastened in the other's body." Gleig finally found his friend, shot through the temple by a rifle bullet. The hole was so small as to leave hardly any evidence of its entrance."[53] Gleig threw himself to the ground and wept like a child.

The next morning a British officer walked over the battlefield and wrote of the dead Americans in his diary, *"These poor fellows presented a strange appearance; their hair, eyebrows, and lashes were thickly covered with hoar-frost, or rime, their bloodless cheeks vying with its whiteness. Few were dressed in military uniforms, and most of them bore the appearance of farmers or husbandmen. Peace to their ashes! They had nobly died in defending their country."[54]*

Both sides claimed victory, especially the British since the attack had been repulsed. What really mattered was that the British staff mistakenly concluded that if the Americans were bold enough to attack, then they must have the 20,000 men reported by some intelligence reports. Based on the boldness of the night attack, they decided not to push towards New Orleans until they were well

BRITTON 01

Left: Rodriquez Canal,
Chalmette National Battlefield.
Photo by Charles Patton, author

Below: Chalmette Battlefield,
looking toward cypress swamp.
Photo by Charles Patton, author.

reinforced. This hesitation eventually closed off any chance of a British victory.

The following day, December 24th, Jackson had every available body digging fortifications along the Rodriquez Canal, six miles south of New Orleans. This canal was an old millrace that stretched about three-quarters of a mile between the cypress swamp and the Mississippi River. Separating the Americans and the British was the *Chalmette Plantation* where the battle would be fought. That same day a peace treaty was signed between the American and British Commissioners; but as requested by the British, it was *not* to be effective until ratified by Parliament and Congress.

The next day, December 25, 1814, a bugle sounded on the eastern side of the British camp near the swamp. A bugle in the British camp answered and a single cannon was fired. General Edward Packenham, personally picked by Wellington, had finally caught up to his command.

It only took General Packenham a couple of hours to see the misfortune he had inherited. In a staff meeting that went late into the night he cursed the fact that he was hemmed in on one side by the Mississippi River and a cypress swamp on the other. What was worse, he had a thin sixty-mile supply line that could only supply him with a limited amount of supplies. But what really galled him was that the advanced guard did not storm New Orleans the first day when they had a chance. It was reported that he was considering pulling out and re-deploying to a more manageable situation. Admiral Cochrane scoffed at him and threatened to storm the American lines with 2,000 British sailors and then, "the army could bring up the baggage." Cochrane's intimidation worked. Although Packenham had a deep distrust of Admiral Cochrane he decided to fight with the hand that was dealt to him.

On December 27, Packenham had naval guns brought in to deal with the American ship, *Carolina*, that was spewing death into their camp. They quickly sank the *Carolina*, but the Americans managed to get the other gunship, the *Louisiana*, to safety. Now Packenham could deal with the Americans ahead of them. That night he moved his army forward and drove in most of the American pickets. Jackson knew something was up and would not rest. For "…five days and four nights he went without sleep and never once sat at a table to take a regular meal. Food was brought to him in the field, and he would pick at what was offered without dismounting."[55]

Because of his sickness with dysentery Jackson constantly walked along the lines instead of riding a horse.

He regularly talked with the officers and troops. Many writers and eyewitness accounts talk about how he personally knew almost every Tennessean there and at least half of the Kentuckians and would call them by name. One day Jackson was talking to some of his soldiers near the far eastern side of his line, near the cypress swamp, when he approached Captain Donelson, a relative of his wife. The General talked with him for a while and then commented that it looked like he had the honor of holding the extreme left of the line. Donelson replied, "No General; [Captain] Jugeat and his damned Choctaws are still to the left of me."

"Don't say 'damned Choctows,' Jack; they are good fellows, and Jugeat, as you know is a trump. But where are they? I don't see them."

"Oh, they're away out in the swamp, basking on logs, like so many alligators!"[56]

Some of the British would have the honor of meeting up with the Choctows when Packenham attacked the next morning with the tactic of "*reconnaissance in force*". He would probe the American lines for weakness and if the opportunity presented itself then he would attack in force. But Jackson now had most of his line prepared. The gunship, *Louisiana,* poured round after round of devastating cannon shot into their mist. One particular shot killed fifteen soldiers. And any soldier who got within range of the rifles of the New Orleans or Tennessee sharpshooters was immediately shot. Lieutenant Gleig again wrote, "we have had frequent cause to acknowledge; but, perhaps, on no occasion did they assert their claim to the title of good artillery men more effectively than on the present. Scarce a ball passed over, or fell short of its mark, but all striking full into the midst of our ranks, occasion[ing] terrible havoc."[57] On the left of Jackson's line near the swamp, some of Packenham's men were closing in on Jackson's line. Just as they were about to charge and turn the line Packenham ordered a withdrawal. The attack was not a success for Packenham but it did point out a weakness on the left side of Jackson's line. But Jackson saw it too and immediately ordered additional men and cannons to be placed there.

Three days later British sailors, by a Herculean feat, managed to bring up fourteen additional cannons from the fleet. Packenham gave the Americans a New Years day awakening with a tremendous cannonade. They had hoped to demolish the earthen fortifications, which the Americans were hiding behind, but it did not work. The cannon balls just sank into the Louisiana mud, causing no damage. The Americans were slow to respond but soon American artillery led by Dominique You, Jean Laffite's brother, were demolishing much of the artillery setup in the battlefield. By noon the British fire slackened noticeably. British artillery crews had a difficult time aiming their guns because they had a tendency to sink in the soft Louisiana soil where the water level was just eighteen inches below the surface. Much of their artillery was damaged and crews killed. Also, because of their extremely long supply line they were running out of powder and cannon balls. The British artillery officers went back to their camp disgusted, while Jean Laffite's Baratarian crew held their heads high.

During the height of the artillery battle a certain Mr. Judah Touro, an American civilian volunteer, was hit in the thigh by a twelve-pound cannon ball leaving a hideous and gaping wound. He was bandaged and laid aside to die. A short time later his business partner and close friend, Mr. Shepherd learned of his friend's wound and came to his aid, abandoning the mission on which Commodore Patterson had sent him. Dr. Ker, the American Chief Surgeon, who was taking care of Touro shook his head and said there was no hope for him. Shepherd immediately loaded Touro into a cart and headed to town, applying him liberally with brandy the whole way. Mr. Touro would later say that this was the only time he ever drank to excess. Mr.

Shepherd left him with some of the ladies of New Orleans and returned to face Commodore Patterson. The Commodore's anger was evident when he returned, but Mr. Shepherd told the Commodore bluntly, "Commodore, you can hang or shoot me, and it will be all right; but my best friend needed my assistance, and nothing on earth could have induced me to neglect him." After relating the details of his absence the Commodore wisely let it pass. Mr. Shepherd and Mr. Touro later became immensely wealthy. When Mr. Touro died in 1854 he left half his fortune to charitable purposes, including $80,000 for a New Orleans Alms House, money for the re-establishment of Zion and contributions to many Jewish synagogues. The other half went to Mr. Shephard, who not needing the additional wealth, spent the money improving the street that they lived on - a project that Touro had long planned. The street name was changed to *Touro Street*.

Two days later on January 3rd, twenty-two hundred Kentucky volunteers arrived by flatboat. This would bring Jackson's army up to 5,400 men. The British had over 10,000. Jackson was ecstatic to see the reinforcements, but he was also shocked. Over 700 hundred of the Kentuckians did not have arms and many of the others only had old fowling pieces. General Jackson was reported as saying, "I don't believe it. I have never seen a Kentuckian without a gun and a pack of cards and a bottle of whiskey in my life!" Jackson had New Orleans scrounged for any firearm but few were found. Anyone without a gun was given a stick to club the enemy with.

Action ceased for a few days while both sides received re-enforcements and strengthened fortifications. British strength rose to 14,000 men while General Jackson made the front line bristle with cannons stripped from the gunship *Louisiana*.

Now Packenham planned his final assault. The plan was to send Major Rennie and his men along the river road and attack the extreme right of the American line. Colonel Thornton would cross the river with fourteen hundred men, come up the west side of the Mississippi River, capture the cannons mounted there and then turn them toward the Americans line raking them with a murderous crossfire. The main thrust would be with 8,000 – 9,000 men who would advance on the far left of Jackson's line near the cypress swamp. This was the point where the December 28th attack had indicated weakness. By coincidence an American deserter had told the British that the Americans were weak there also.

General Jackson had noted that it was a weak point and had strengthened it with a concentration of General Carroll's Tennesseans and more cannons. Also General Adair and his Kentuckians were formed behind General Carroll as a reserve to go where they were needed most. They had anticipated that it would be right in front of Carroll's men. And luckily they were right. Jackson now had his army arrayed as he wanted it. The Louisiana regiments under General Humbert covered the western side of the line near the river, General Carroll's Tennesseans held the middle, while General Coffee's men held the eastern swampy end. Behind Carroll were 2,000 Kentuckians, and behind them were 270 mounted cavalry in case the British broke through the lines. Behind them all were troops and pickets to stop or shoot any American who fled the battle.

"If I were an American, as I am an Englishman,
While a foreign troop was landed in my country, I
never would lay down my arms – never, never, never."
-William Pitt, Earl of Chatham

Chapter Six

Our Lady of Prompt Succor

On the afternoon of January 7th, Commodore Patterson and Mr. Shepherd walked down the western side of the Mississippi River to determine what the British were up to. What the Commodore saw made his blood run cold. The British were pulling boats down the Villeré Canal in order to launch them across the river for an attack on the western side of the river. Patterson knew they were not ready for this. General Morgan, responsible for defense of the western bank, had picked a poor line of defense. He had his few ill-equipped men stretched out too far to do any good. The British would blow right through them and come for his cannons on the west bank. He sent Shepherd with the information to warn Jackson and ask for re-enforcements.

On the evening of January 7th, many of the women of the town were praying for deliverance at the Ursuline Convent in New Orleans. Mother Marie deVezin took the unusual step of bringing the statue of *Our Lady of Prompt Succor* from the nuns' choir to the main altar. She made a vow, in the name of the community, that if her prayers for the city's deliverance were answered a mass of thanksgiving would be offered on the anniversary of the great day forever after.

Very late that evening Mr. Shepherd arrived at General Jackson's headquarters with Commodore Patterson's message of a major attack on the west bank. Jackson said that Patterson was wrong and that the major attack would be in front of General Carroll's men. After first denying re-enforcement to General Morgan on the west bank he reconsidered and sent a few hundred soldiers. It would not be near enough.

On the morning of January 8th General Jackson had been up since 2:00 am consulting with his generals, talking with his men, and drinking coffee with the Lafitte's pirates. At 8:00 am two congreve rockets went up from the British lines signaling the attack to begin. Although the Americans suspected the main attack was imminent, it let them know that the assault was under way, since the battlefield was blanketed with fog.

Colonel Thornton could get only get a third of his boats to the river. Therefore only 440 of 1400 men crossed

Left. Statue of *Our Lady of Prompt Succor*. Used with permission of Archdiocese of New Orleans and the nuns of the Ursuline Convent of New Orleans. Photo by Frank Methe of the *Clarion Herald*.

Below. Ursuline Convent, which nursed the wounded of both sides. Sisters offer prayers each year for our American victory. Located in French Quarter, New Orleans, as convent appears today. Photo by Charles Patton, author,

This stained glass window is from St. Mary's Church on Chartres
Street in New Orleans. The lower portion of the window depicts the
Battle of New Orleans and is used with permission of the Archdiocese
of New Orleans. Photo by Frank Methe of the *Clarion Herald*.

to the west bank. To further aggravate his problem the current in the Mississippi River pushed the boats so far down stream that they landed several miles south of their intended landing point, putting them even further behind the attack schedule. His men were still crossing the river when the signal rockets were launched.

As planned, Major Rennie rushed his men up the river road while General Gibbs started the assault on the left side of Jackson's line. General Keane was with the reserves and would send them where he thought necessary. Among these reserves were the fabled 93rd Sutherland Highlanders. This regiment totaled about 1,000 men commanded by Colonel Dale. They were comprised of men no less than six feet tall. Their uniforms were rich and showy. They were conspicuously religious, even paying for a chaplain out of their own pockets to accompany them. When in South Africa, they did community projects and sent money home for charitable and religious purposes. Wherever they went in England, they aroused the local interest. The Highlanders, up until that time, were normally kept at home or at a safe posting because of the interest that England showed in them.

Major Rennie's men rushed out of the fog along the river road and surprised the Americans near an isolated redoubt jutting out from the American line. The Americans fell back toward the main line but the Americans and British were so mixed that the men along the main line could not fire into them. When the last man got back across General Humbert ordered Beale's Rifles, a crack New Orleans rifle group, to fire at Rennie and his men. Major Rennie and all his officers were killed immediately. General Humbert now ordered all his Louisiana regiments to fire. An American officer, in an oration years after the battle said, "the right flank of Rennie's column seemed to sink into the earth." While they were getting devastating fire from the Louisiana ranks, Commodore Patterson opened a deadly cannon fire from the western bank of the Mississippi River. What was left of Rennie's men retreated as best they could.

Disaster was happening on the other side of the battlefield where the main thrust had been directed. As the troops approached, cannon fire ripped the British lines. Lt. Gleig wrote, "[We] were mowed down by the hundreds. Several times the column halted, only to re-form and start forward again."[58] One cannon filled to the brim with musket balls and chain hit the head of a column at point blank range. It was estimated later that two hundred men were either killed or wounded in this one blast.

The battlefield at Chalmette on January 8, 1815. Five miles below New Orleans on the left bank of the Mississippi. Monochrome aquatint by H. Laclotte. Used with permission of the Historic New Orleans.Collection., accession no.1971-53

One British officer described the sound of the American cannons, "...the echo from the cannonade and musketry was so tremendous in the [cypress] forests that the vibration seemed as if the earth was cracking and tumbling to pieces, or as if the heavens were rent asunder by the most terrific peals of thunder that ever rumbled; it was the most awful and the grandest mixture of sounds to be conceived; the woods seemed to crack to an interminable distance, each cannon report was answered one hundredfold, and produced an intermingled roar, surpassing strange...this phenomenon can neither be fancied nor described, save by those who can bear evidence of the fact...and the flashes of fire looked as if coming out of the bowels of the earth, so little above its surface were the batteries of the Americans."[59]

As the British troops got close enough to think about storming the American lines they discovered that Colonel Mullens' regiment had forgotten the facines and ladders needed to storm the ramparts. Now they halted, not knowing what to do. This was fatal for them. They were standing in front of the American lines trying to fire back but not advancing. Rifle and musket fire mowed them down by the hundreds. General Coffee said, "Before they reached our small arms, our grape and canister mowed down whole columns, but that was nothing to the carnage of our Rifles and muskets."[60] One of Packenham's aides, Major Harry Smith said that he, "never saw a more destructive fire poured upon a single line of men."[61]

The British troops could take no more. They broke and ran. General Gibbs screamed at his men to reform but they did not listen. General Packenham was waiting with General Lambert and the reserves. Packenham turned and said, "Lambert, that's a terrific fire!" He then spurred his horse and rushed into the unfolding disaster where he was met by General Gibbs. Gibbs almost sobbingly, shouted to Packenham, "The troops will not obey me. They will not follow."[62]

A couple of months earlier, on the day before Packenham sailed for Louisiana, a friend of his expressed concern for his safety and reminded him not to expose himself unnecessarily to enemy fire. Packenham replied, "I promise you that I will not unnecessarily expose myself to the fire of the enemy, but you are too old and good a soldier not to be aware that a case might arise in which the Commander-in-Chief may find it absolutely necessary to place himself at the head of his troops in the hottest fire and by his own personal conduct encourage them to victory. If this happens, I must not flinch, though death be my lot."[63]

Battle of New Orleans, *Ballout's Pictorial Drawing Room Companion.* Used courtesy of the Historic New Orleans Collection, Museum Research Center. Accession number 1958.98.6.

The Battle of New Orleans. Engraving by Thomas Phillibrown of painting by D.M.Carter. Courtesy of Historic New Orleans Collection, Museum/Research Center. Accession number 1951.43.1

Battle for New Orleans Jan. 8, 1815, Courtesy of Historic New Orleans Collection, Museum/Research Center. Accession number 1959.160.12

Death of General Packenham. Engraving by Yeager, after West. Permission for use obtained from the Hermitage: Home of President Andrew Jackson

Packenham rushed toward the panic stricken and retreating troops.

On the other side of the field General Keane ordered Scotland's pride and England's interest, the 93rd Highlanders, to go to the support of General Gibbs' troops. Colonel Dale, their commander, turned to the regimental doctor, handed him his watch and a letter and said, "Give these to my wife; I shall die at the head of my regiment."[64]

As General Packenham reached his troops and started rallying his men he turned to one of his aides and said, "Order up the reserve."[65] The bugler started to raise the bugle to his lips when a cannon filled with grape shot ripped through his arm and the bugle fell to the ground. The same cannon shot also killed Packenham's horse and ripped open the General's thigh. Packenham mounted a second horse and again was shot out of the saddle. Captain McDougal caught him as he rolled off the horse. This must have been a bitter moment for McDougal, since he had also caught General Ross when he was killed near Baltimore. As Packenham was picked up by fellow officers, another shot hit him in the groin and he lost consciousness. Years later Andrew Jackson wrote President Monroe, *"I heard a single rifle shot from a group of country carts we had been using, and a moment thereafter I saw Packenham reel and pitch out of his saddle. I always believed he fell from the bullet of a free man of color, who was a famous rifle shot and came from the Attakapas region of Louisiana.*"[66]

A moment later General Gibbs was mortally wounded. Seconds later General Keane was wounded in the groin but lived.

Marching into hell from the other side of the battlefield were the 93rd Highlanders. The bagpipers were playing the *Monymusk*, the regimental charge. They started with about 1000 men. As they neared the American lines cannon and rifle fire exacted a tremendous toll. Colonel Dale was quickly identified as an officer and killed. The regiment halted in front of the awful fire coming from the American ramparts. The second in command would not order retreat until he received word from a higher ranking authority, so they just stood there and took the deadly fire. An American later said, "It was an act of cool determined bravery." Word finally came for retreat and that night at roll call only 250 answered. The regiment had 550 killed and another 200 wounded.

One small group of British soldiers managed to reach the American ramparts. Major Wilkinson and Lt. Lavack had about twenty men with them as they tried to climb up the rampart toward the Americans. Major

Wilkinson pulled himself atop the rampart, stood up and was riddled with bullets. As Lt. Lavack reached the top, some American officers had the men to hold their fire and approached him. Lavak demanded their swords. They laughed at him and said, "Oh, no; you are alone, and, therefore ought to surrender yourself our prisoner."[67] Lt. Lavick looked around and saw that his men had thrown themselves down in the ditch for protection. His head and shoulders slumped in dejection and then meekly surrendered without resistance.

General Lambert, who was now in command, wrote in his report to Lord Bathurst that the destruction of the high command, "caused a wavering in the column which in such a situation became irreparable."[68] Lambert, who had been in charge of the reserves, could only cover the retreat of the fleeing soldiers in front of him. It had been only thirty minutes since the first charge and now it was all over.

But it was not quite over. On the other side of the Mississippi River Colonel Thornton had easily broken through the ill-armed and poorly positioned forces of General Morgan of Kentucky. The Americans on the west bank were in full retreat. When Commodore Patterson saw them fleeing and the British soldiers coming for his guns, he ordered that the cannons be spiked and the powder thrown into the river. While Thornton's men were trying to unspike the cannons he received word from General Lambert of the disaster on the other side of the river and a request for him to withdraw his troops.

Two hours after the battle had begun General Andrew Jackson stepped up on the ramparts to survey the battlefield. Jackson later said, "I never had so grand and awful an idea of the resurrection as on that day. After the smoke of the battle had cleared off somewhat, I saw in the distance more than five hundred Britons emerging from the heaps of their dead comrades"[69] coming forth to surrender.

The British had lost 2,037 men killed, wounded, or captured. The Americans lost 13 killed and 39 wounded.

Chapter Seven

Victory is Ours

Back at the cathedral in the Ursuline Convent, Sunday morning mass was being held with the sounds of the battle only six miles away. The church was full of scared people. The nuns and women of the town had spent the night in the church praying. Many felt that the church would protect them from any marauding British soldiers. Mass was not yet finished and at the very moment of communion a courier burst into the cathedral shouting with his voice full of emotion, "Victory is ours!" Bedlam broke loose in the church but was quickly restored and the *Te Deum* was sung.

The tremendous lopsided victory at Chalmette has always appeared to the people of New Orleans and to Andrew Jackson as bordering on the supernatural. Although General Jackson was not a church going person he considered the event as a "signal interposition of heaven" and asked Father Du Bourg to order "a service of public thanksgiving to be performed in the Cathedral in token... of the great assistance we have received from the ruler of all events, and our humble sense of it."

On January 9th, the day after the battle and sixteen days *after* the signing of the peace treaty, Major General Johnston of the British Army left England for Bermuda with reinforcements and the following orders, *"You will notify your arrival by the speediest opportunity to Major General Sir Edward Packenham...You...will hold your Troops in readiness to execute his orders and to proceed to whatever Place He shall direct... "[70]* General Johnston's job was to help occupy and hold the Louisiana Territory from counterstrikes.

On January 19th, as the British were evacuating the last of their troops, a British medical officer, a Dr.Wadsdale, came forward under a flag of truce with a letter from General Lambert. The letter stated that his army had departed and that he had left to Jackson's care a few doctors and some eighty soldiers who were too wounded to be evacuated. Jackson and his surgeon-general, Dr. Ker, visited the British hospital at Jumonville (the plantation at the back of the British encampment) and assured the wounded that they would be well taken care of. "The circumstances of these wounded men being made known in the city, a number of ladies rode down in their carriages with such articles as were deemed essential to the comforts of the unfortunates. One of these ladies was a belle of the city, Miss Manette Trudeau...who was famed for her charms of person and mind. Seeing her noble philanthropy and devotion to his countrymen, Dr. Josiah E. Kerr, one of the British surgeons left behind to care for the wounded, conceived a warm regard and admiration for her which subsequent acquaintance ripened into love. Dr. Kerr settled in New Orleans after the war and [married] the charming Creole, whose acquaintance he had made under such interesting circumstances, and became one of the leading professional men of the city...(This Dr. Kerr is not to be confused with Dr. David C. Ker, Jackson's surgeon-general)."[71]

For the remainder of the wounded, the Ursuline Convent opened its doors as a hospital for all the wounded British and Americans. So thankful were the soldiers of their kind treatment, that when they were sufficiently healed and it was time to leave, British veterans wept like children. The men of Tennessee and Kentucky were so grateful that for years they sent baskets filled with bacon, fruits and other gifts as tokens of their gratitude to the Ursuline nuns.

As Mother Marie de Vezin promised, a Mass is still held every January 8th in thanksgiving for the deliverance of New Orleans. It is held under the watchful eye of the statue of *Our Lady of Prompt Succor*

On January 23rd General Jackson marched his soldiers into New Orleans for the celebration and thanksgiving mass. "...the streets were jammed. Balconies and rooftops were alive with spectators. People gathered everywhere: in the great square opposite the cathedral that fronted the river, in the streets leading to the square, and along the levee. The uniformed companies of Plauché's battalion formed two lines from the entrance of the square to the church. A temporary arch was erected in the middle of the square, opposite the main entrance of the cathedral. The arch was supported by six Corinthian columns, and on each side of it stood a young lady – one represented Justice, the other Liberty. Under the arch, standing on a pedestal, were two children holding a laurel crown. Between the arch and the cathedral "the most beautiful girls" took positions at regular intervals, each representing a different state or territory of the Union, all dressed in white with transparent blue veils and a silver star on their foreheads. Each held in her right hand a flag inscribed with the name of the state she represented and in her left hand a basket of flowers. A lance embedded in the ground behind each young lady carried a shield with the name of a state or territory. The shields, linked together with garlands of evergreens and flowers, filled the distance from the arch to the cathedral....Then through the gates of the plaza, strode the Hero of the Battle of New Orleans, accompanied by his staff. An enormous cheer burst from the crowd. People waved to him and called him by name. Repeated salvos of artillery announced his presence and saluted his magnificent accomplishment. Entering the square, Jackson was requested to proceed to the cathedral by the walk prepared for him. As he passed under the arch the two children lowered the laurel crown to his head...At the porch of the cathedral the Abbé Dubourg...welcomed Jackson with a speech glowing with praise to the Almighty for having sent the country such a sublime savior...Then he handed the General a bough of consecrated laurel. The crowd hushed to hear Jackson's reply. 'Reverend Sir, I receive with gratitude and pleasure the symbolical crown which piety has prepared; I receive it in the name of the brave men who have so effectually seconded my exertions for the preservation of their country'....After a few more sentences…Jackson concluded by wishing the city wealth and happiness commensurate with its courage…"[72]

The congregations started singing the *Te Deum* which, was picked up by the people outside the cathedral, who were standing in the courtyard and the surrounding streets. Jackson was then escorted out with an honor guard.

Later that week at a grand ball held for the great victory, Vincent Nolte described General Jackson and his wife Rachel, who had just arrived, dancing at the ball. "To see these two figures, the General, a long, haggard man, with limbs like a skeleton, and Madame la Generale, a short fat dumpling, bobbing opposite each other like half-drunken Indians, to the wild melody of *'Possum up de Gum Tree'*, and [then] endeavoring to make a spring into the air, was very remarkable, and far more…[an entertaining]… spectacle than any European ballet could possibly have furnished."[73]

Chapter Eight

But Providence ordained it otherwise and we must submit

On the East Coast of America, people waited in dread of the news. Doom and despair pervaded every thought of every American. Everyone knew that New Orleans was under attack. A New England Federalist newspaper proclaimed, "We are a lost country. A wicked administration has ruined us"…"It was not an over statement …to say that there was not one well informed man in the northern states who believed that New Orleans could be successfully defended." [74]

The gloom around Washington was extremely thick. Washington had been burned, the treasury was broke, and delegates from the New England states were on their way to Washington demanding constitution revisions as the price for their continued acceptance of the Union. On January 23, 1815, word reached Washington about the naval loss on Lake Borgne and the "Night Battle" in New Orleans.

A severe snowstorm stopped all travel going in and out of Washington for ten days, blocking any news of New Orleans. Every soul in Washington was worn out with mere hunger for news. A Federalist newspaper printed, "It is merely a question of time; the next mail will finish New Orleans and *you*!" [75]

A young visitor visiting Washington was asked to dine with President Madison and his wife Dolley at the Octagon House, temporary quarters for the President. He wrote of it to his father stating, *"The president... appeared not to know all his guests, even by name. For some time there was silence, or very few words. The President and Mrs. Madison made one or two commonplace remarks to me and others. After a few moments a servant came in and whispered to Mr. Madison, who went out, followed by his Secretary. It was mentioned about the room that the Southern mail had arrived, and a rather unseemly anxiety was expressed about the fate of New Orleans, of whose imminent danger we heard last night. The President soon returned, with added gravity, and said that there was no news! Silence ensued. No man seemed to know what to say at such a crisis, and, I suppose, from the fear of saying what might not be acceptable, said nothing at all.*[76]

On February 4th an express rider from New Orleans finally pushed his way through the deep snow with the astounding news of Jackson's victory.

"Glory be to God...Glory to Jackson...Glory to the militia... Sons of Freedom...benefactors of your country... all hail", exclaimed *the Niles Weekly Register.*

The *National Intelligencer* in their largest type shouted, **"ALMOST INCREDIBLE VICTORY !!!"**

Washington went wild with the "maddest enthusiasm". People erupted from their homes and danced in the streets. They thronged the President and his staff and showered them with congratulations. "Soon after night-fall members of Congress and others, ...presented themselves at the President's house. At eight o'clock it was crowded to its full capacity, Mrs. Madison (the President being with the Cabinet) did the honors of the occasion. And what a happy scene it was! Among the large proportion present ...of both Houses of Congress were gentlemen of most opposite politics, ...[but] now with elated spirits thanking God, and with softened hearts...But the most conspicuous object in the room, *the observed of all observers*, was Mrs. Madison herself, then in the meridian of life and queenly beauty...No one could doubt who beheld the radiance of joy which lighted up her countenance and diffused its beams around, that all uncertainty was at an end, and that the government of the country had in very truth... *'passed from gloom to glory.'* With a grace, all her own, to her visitors she reciprocated heartfelt congratulations upon the glorious and happy change in the aspect of public affairs; dispensing with liberal hand, to every individual in the large assembly, the proverbial hospitalities of that house..."[77]

The news rocketed north to Philadelphia and New York where people were equally exuberant. In Philadelphia no one wanted to be by themselves. Men, women and children danced in the streets, weeping with tears streaming down their faces. So sure had they been of their young nation's destruction that this seemed like a miraculous gift from God. An illumination was made of Jackson with the saying, "This day shall ne'er go by, from this day to the ending of the world, but He, in it, shall be remembered. In fact, for the next fifty years, January 8th was as big an event as the 4th of July and was remembered in parades and celebrations every year until after the Civil War.

In the Gulf Coast the British fleet was rushing to Fort Bowyer's at Mobile to attempt to rectify their defeat and capture what they could before word of the peace treaty could reach them. They did capture Fort Bowyers but a ship soon brought word of the peace treaty and ratification. Now England was caught in their own trap. The treaty had been designed to give the British troops enough time to capture New Orleans and Louisiana and not to give the Americans enough time to respond. Now the expeditionary force was woefully behind schedule. They had a huge army off the coast of the southern United States and they could not exploit the capture of Mobile as they were forbidden to do so by their own handiwork, which they had worked into the treaty. So when word of the treaty officially reached them they packed up and sailed home. This not only ended their dream of gaining a great territory in the New World, but without the intended enforced buffer zone between the whites and Indians the future of the American Indian was doomed.

Nine days after word reached Washington of Jackson's victory, word came of the peace agreement in Ghent. Again people paraded in the streets shouting, "Peace! Peace!"

In New York a Mr.Goodrich wrote of the effect the news had on the city, *"It was about eight o'clock on Saturday evening that the tidings circulated through the city. In half an hour after the news reached the wharf, Broadway was one living sea of shouting, rejoicing people. 'Peace! Peace! Peace!' was the deep, harmonious, universal anthem. The whole spectacle was enlivened by a sudden inspiration. Somebody came with a torch; the bright idea passed into a thousand brains. In a few minutes thousands and tens of thousands of people were marching about with candles, lamps, torches-making the jubilant street appear like a gay and gorgeous procession. The whole night Broadway sang its song of peace. We were all democrats, all federalists! Old enemies rushed into each other's arms; every house was in a revel; every heart seemed melted by a joy which banished all evil thought and feeling. Nobody asked that happy night what were the terms of the treaty: we had got peace, that was enough! I moved about for hours in the ebbing and flowing tide of people, not being aware that I had opened my lips. The next morning I found that I was hoarse from having joined in the exulting cry of 'peace, peace!'*[78]

Victory and peace had come so quickly in succession that, "people tended to fuse the two events together. The result was the feeling that Andrew Jackson had come like some special messenger of the Almighty to rescue His people and preserve their freedom. Small wonder that Jackson's place in the pride and affection of the American people lasted until his death – and beyond…his popularity exceed[ing] that of Washington, Jefferson or Franklin."[79] For the rest of Jackson's life, wherever he would go, "women, children and old men would line the road to look at him as they would an elephant."[80]

"Who is not proud to feel himself an American - our wrongs revenged - our rights recognized!", said Congressman Charles Ingersoll of Pennsylvania, expressing the sentiments of almost every American.[81]

Even Thomas Jefferson, who had profound misgivings about Andrew Jackson's character, toasted him by saying, "Honor and gratitude to those who have filled the measure of their country's honor."[82]

President Madison wrote Thomas Jefferson, "[The] affair at New Orleans was a better guarantee of peace than the parchment document of Ghent"[83]

Congress had a gold medal struck commemorating Jackson and the Battle of New Orleans. The face of the medal shows a profile of Jackson but the back of the coin reflects the two remarkable events as it was imprinted on the mind of every living American at that time. In artistic symbolism, it shows a lady representing *Victory* writing the word *Orleans* onto a tablet when she is interrupted by another lady, representing *Peace*. In the early 1900's it was found in a pawnshop, purchased and donated to the *American Numismatic Society* in New York City where it resides today.

In Ireland, the Whig press greeted the news of the New Orleans disaster with satisfied gloom. They pointed out that, "the best officers on both sides at New Orleans were Irish – Packenham and Keane for the English, Generals Jackson and Coffey for America. The battle was almost a local affair."[84]

One British newspaper stated that they had not expected the Louisiana Frenchmen to be loyal to the United States and had expected their help in the campaign, but "they were with the Americans to a man."[85]

In London the news was met with disbelief and quickly swept under the rug, which was easy to do since Napoleon was on the loose again. Generals Packenham's and Gibb's bodies were shipped home in barrels of rum for preservation and given a decent funeral. A statue of Packenham and Gibbs was erected in St. Paul's Cathedral in London.

From Brussels the Duke of Wellington wrote to General Packenham's brother, lambasting Admiral

Statue honoring General Andrew Jackson.
Jackson Square, New Orleans. Photo by
Charles Patton, author.

Night photograph of beautiful plaza with statue honoring General Andrew Jackson. Jackson Square, New Orleans, Photo by Charles Patton, author

Cochrane, *"My dear Langford, I have received your letter of the 18th and I am very much obliged to you and highly gratified by your poor brother's recollection of me...We have but one consolation, that he fell as he lived in the honourable discharge of his duty; and distinguished [himself] as a soldier and as a man. I cannot but regret however that he was ever employed on such a service or with such a colleague. The expedition to New Orleans originated with that colleague and plunder was its object. I knew and stated in July that the transports could not approach within leagues of the landing place; and enquired [as to] what means were provided to enable a sufficient body of troops with their artillery, provisions and stores to land, and afterwards communicate with them.*

*Then as plunder was the object, the Admiral took care to be attended by a sufficient number of **sharks** to carry the plunder off from a place at which he knew well he could not remain. The secret of the expedition was thus communicated, and in this manner this evil design defeated it own end. The Americans were prepared with an Army in a fortified position which still would have been carried if the duties of others, that is of the Admiral, had been as well performed as that of him whom we lament.*

But Providence ordained it otherwise and we must submit....Believe me, Ever yours most affectionately, Wellington. "[86]

For England and the United States, "a century would pass before the breach was fully healed and another fifty years and two world wars were required to forge and temper an enduring friendship. It is not entirely fanciful to suppose that the seeds of that friendship were sown on the [battle]field of Chalmette, on January 8th, 1815, when armies of the United States and Britain faced each other in battle for the last time."[87]

The End

Advance our waving colors on the walls,
*Rescued is **Orleans** from the English wolves"*
-Shakespeare, Henry VI

Epilogue

Even after the defeat at New Orleans, the British never gave up in their hopes of reigning in America's growing power. Thirty years later when Jackson was in his last couple of years at the Hermitage, and campaigning to get Congress to annex Texas to the Union, the British were still trying to curtail America's growing power. Congress had denied Texas annexation three different times and the Texans had just about had enough. Jackson was trying to save the day and doing his best to make annexation happen while British diplomats were all over Texas, promising aid and doing anything they could think of to keep Texas from joining the union. But Jackson and President Polk finally got annexation through Congress. One congressional opposition leader finally gave in and said that he could not fight a sitting President and Andrew Jackson at the same time.

Feelings between England and the United States healed somewhat through the years, and finally started healing in earnest during WWI, but I don't believe it was until WWII that we truly became friends. Winston Churchill (whose mother was an American) dealt with this antagonistic feeling on August 20th, 1940. Knowing that England had to have America's support to survive the upcoming struggle, he addressed the House of Commons and made the following comment:

"These two great organizations of the English-speaking democracies, the British Empire and the United States, will have to be somewhat mixed up together in some of their affairs for mutual and general advantage. For my own part, looking out upon the future, I do not view the process with any misgivings. I could not stop it if I wished; no one can stop it. Like the Mississippi, it just keeps rolling along. Let it roll. Let it roll on full flood, inexorable, irresistible, benignant, to broader lands and better days."

-*Winston Churchill*
April 20, 1940

Chalmette Monument. The cornerstone of this monument honoring the American victory at New Orleans was laid in 1840, shortly after a visit to the site by Andrew Jackson. The monument was completed in 1908. Photo by Charles Patton, author.

ENDNOTES

[1] Adams to Jay, July 19, 1785; *Works of John Adams, VIII*, p.282

[2] Adams to Jay, Aug. 6, 1785; *Works of John Adams, VIII*, p.290-291

[3] Adams to Jay, Nov.30, 1787; *Works of John Adams, VIII*, p.463

[4] *The Diplomacy of the War of 1812*, Updike, p.28

[5] *Writings of Thomas Jefferson*, VIII, 143-147

[6] Bonaparte, First Council, to the Marquis Francois De Barbemarbois, and Marshal Louis Alexandre Berthier, Ministers of Finance and War, Easter Sunday, April 10, 1803 at St. Cloud

[7] *The Pictorial Field-Book of the War of 1812*, Lossing, p.133

[8] *The British at the Gates*, Reilly, p.6

[9] *The British at the Gates*, Reilly, p.5

[10] *The Course of American Democracy*, Remini, p.212, John Hopkins Univ. Press, Originally by Harper & Row

[11] *The Struggle for the Gulf Borderlands*, Owsley, p.12

[12] *The Struggle for the Gulf Borderlands*, Owsley, p.12

[13] *The Struggle for the Gulf Borderlands*, Owsley, p.19

[14] *The Struggle for the Gulf Borderlands*, Owsley, p.28

[15] *The Course of American Empire*, Remini, p.214, John Hopkins Univ. Press, Originally by Harper & Row

[16] *The Struggle for the Gulf Borderlands*, Owsley, p.84

[17] *The Course of American Empire*, Remini, p.218, John Hopkins Univ. Press, Originally by Harper & Row

[18] *The Struggle for the Gulf Borderlands*, Owsley, p.84

[19] *The Course of American Empire*, Remini, p.224, John Hopkins Univ. Press, Originally by Harper & Row

[20] *The Baratarians and the Battle of New Orleans*, de Grummond, p.26

[21] *The Baratarians and the Battle of New Orleans*, de Grummond, p.x

[22] *The British at the Gates*, Reilly, p.150

[23] *The British at the Gates*, Reilly, p.49

[24] *The Burning of Washington*, Pitch, p.149

[25] *The Pictorial Field-Book of the War of 1812*, Lossing, p.933-934

[26] *The Burning of Washington*, Pitch, p.139-140

[27] *The Burning of Washington*, Pitch, p.142

[28] *The Story of Horseshoe Bend National Military Park*, Martin, p.27

[29] *The Course of American Empire*, Remini, p.244, John Hopkins Univ. Press, Originally by Harper & Row

[30] *The Course of American Empire*, Remini, p.243, John Hopkins Univ. Press, Originally by Harper & Row

[31] *The Course of American Empire*, Remini, p.245, John Hopkins Univ. Press, Originally by Harper & Row

[32] *Battle of New Orleans Sesquicentennial Celebration*, p.86

[33] *The Baratarians and the Battle of New Orleans*, de Grummond, p.30-31

[34] *The British at the Gates*, Reilly, p.335

[35] *The Baratarians and the Battle of New Orleans*, de Grummond, p.30-31

[36] *The Baratarians and the Battle of New Orleans*, de Grummond, p.30-31

[37] Liverpool to Castlereagh, Dec.23, 1814; Wellington's Supplementary Despatches, IX., p.495

[38] *Jackson and New Orleans*, Walker, p.58

[39] *Battle of New Orleans Sesquicentennial Celebration*, p.151

[40] *The Baratarians and the Battle of New Orleans*, de Grummond, p.35

[41] *The Battle of New Orleans*, Viking Press, Remini p.56

[42] *The Course of American Empire*, Remini, p.254, John Hopkins Univ. Press, Originally by Harper & Row

[43] *The Course of American Empire*, Remini, p.254, John Hopkins Univ. Press, Originally by Harper & Row

[44] *Life of Andrew Jackson*, Vol. II, Parton, p.70

[45] *Life of Andrew Jackson*, Vol. II, Parton, p.69

[46] *The Battle of New Orleans*, Viking Press, Remini p.70

[47] *The Battle of New Orleans*, Viking Press, Remini p.72

[48] *The Course of American Empire*, Remini, p.264, John Hopkins Univ. Press, Originally by Harper & Row

[49] *Life of Andrew Jackson*, Parton, Vol. II, p.77

[50] *History of Andrew Jackson*, Buell, p.357-358 [Buell has a reputation of making up his own quotes and this may be the case here, but I have included it because it reflected the general feeling of the Americans along the frontier.]

[51] *Life of Andrew Jackson*, Parton, p.96

[52] *The Baratarians and the Battle of New Orleans*, de Grummond, p.92

[53] *The Battle of New Orleans*, Viking Press, Remini p.82

[54] *Life of Andrew Jackson*, Parton, Vol. II, p.107

[55] *The Battle of New Orleans*, Viking Press, Remini p.82

[56] *History of Andrew Jackson*, Buell, p.403 [Again Buell's quotes are questionable. General Coffee and his men historically held the far eastern end of the swamp.]

[57] *The Battle of New Orleans*, Viking Press, Remini p.96

[58] *The Battle of New Orleans*, Viking Press, Remini p.146

[59] *Life of Andrew Jackson*, Parton, p.203-204

[60] *The Course of American Empire*, Remini, p.279, John Hopkins Univ. Press, Originally by Harper & Row

[61] *The Course of American Empire*, Remini, p.278, John Hopkins Univ. Press, Originally by Harper & Row

[62] *The Course of American Empire*, Remini, p.278, John Hopkins Univ. Press, Originally by Harper & Row

[63] *Major General Sir Edward M. Packenham*, Valerie McNain Scott, Lady Packenham, p.36

[64] *The Battle of New Orleans*, Viking Press, Remini p.139

[65] *The Course of American Empire*, Remini, p.279, John Hopkins Univ. Press, Originally by Harper & Row

[66] *Negro Soldiers in the Battle of New Orleans*, Marcus Christian, p.41

[67] *The Battle of New Orleans*, Viking Press, Remini p.151

[68] *The Battle of New Orleans*, Viking Press, Remini p.150

[69] *The Course of American Empire*, Remini, p.284, John Hopkins Univ. Press, Originally by Harper & Row

[70] *Battle of New Orleans Sesquicentennial Celebration*, p.152

[71] *1915 Centennial Program of the Battle of New Orleans*, Stanley Arthur Clisby, p.282

[72] *The Course of American Empire*, Remini, p.290-292, John Hopkins Univ. Press, Originally by Harper & Row

[73] *Life of Andrew Jackson*, Vol. II, Parton, p.324

[74] *Life of Andrew Jackson*, Parton, Vol. II, p.244

[75] *Life of Andrew Jackson*, Parton, Vol. II p.246

[76] *Dolley Madison – Her Life and Times*, Anthony, p237

[77] *Life of Andrew Jackson*, Parton, Vol. II p.252

[78] *Life of Andrew Jackson*, Parton, Vol. II p.253-254

[79] *The Course of American Empire*, Remini, p.295, John Hopkins Univ. Press, Originally by Harper & Row

[80] *The Course of American Empire*, Remini, p.318, John Hopkins Univ. Press, Originally by Harper & Row

[81] *The Course of American Empire*, Remini, p.295, John Hopkins Univ. Press, Originally by Harper & Row

[82] *The Course of American Empire*, Remini, p.320, John Hopkins Univ. Press, Originally by Harper & Row

[83] *Dolley Madison – Her Life and Times*, Anthony, p239

[84] *Major General Sir Edward M. Packenham*, Valerie McNain Scott, Lady Packenham, p.46

[85] *The Struggle for the Gulf Borderlands*, Owsley, p.168

[86] *Major General Sir Edward M. Packenham*, Valerie McNain Scott, Lady Packenham, p.47

[87] *The British at the Gates*, Reilly, p.5

BIBLIOGRAPHY

Adams to Jay, July 19, 1785; *Works of John Adams, VIII*

Anthony, *Dolley Madison – Her Life and Times*, Doubleday & Co., 1949

Battle of New Orleans Sesquicentennial Celebration, Battle of New Orleans Sesquicentennial Celebration Commission, U.S. Gov't Printing Office, 1965

Buell Augustus C., *History of Andrew Jackson, Vol. I & II,* Charles Scribner's Sons, 1904

DeGrummand, Jane Lucus, *The Baratarians and the Battle of New Orleans,* Louisiana State University Press, 1961

Keats, John, *Eminent Domains,* Charterhouse, New York, 1973

Lossing, Benton L., *The Pictorial Field-Book of the War of 1812,* Harper & Bros., 1868

Marcus Christian, *Negro Soldiers in the Battle of New Orleans,* Battle of New Orleans Anniversary Committee of Louisiana, 1965

Stanley Arthur Clisby, *1915 Centennial Program of the Battle of New Orleans,* Louisiana Historical Society

Martin, Thomas W., *The Story of Horseshoe Bend National Military Park,* Southern University Press at Birmingham, 1959

Owsley, Frank L., *The Struggle for the Gulf Borderlands,* Univ. of Florida Press, 1981

Valerie McNain Scott, Lady Packenham, *Major General Sir Edward M. Packenham,* Battle of New Orleans Anniversary Committee of Louisiana, 1965

Parton, James, *Life of Andrew Jackson*, Vol. II, Mason Bros., 1964

Pitch, Anthony *The Burning of Washington,* Naval Institute Press, 1959

Reilly, Robin, *The British at the Gates,* G.P. Putnam's Sons, New York, 1974

Remini, Robert V*., The Battle of New Orleans*, Viking Press, 1999

Remini, Robert V*., The Course of American Empire*, John Hopkins Univ. Press, Originally by Harper & Row, 1981

Remini, Robert V., *The Course of American Democracy*, John Hopkins Univ. Press, Originally by Harper & Row, 1981

Updyke, Frank, *Diplomacy of the War of 1812,* John Hopkins Press, 1915

Walker, Alexander, *Jackson and New Orleans,* John E. Potter & Co., 1867

Wellington, Liverpool to Castlereagh, Dec.23, 1814; Wellington's Supplementary Despatches, IX.

Additional Credits

The coin on the front and back covers represents a gold medal engraved by Moritz Furst and is used with permission of the American Numismatic Society, New York City.

We are indebted to the Fine Art Students at Western Kentucky University who created the following illustrations for this book.

Joyce Britton – the illustrations opposite pages – 15, 30, 62, and 8.6

Gregory Leppert – the illustrations opposite pages – 20, 50, 54 and 74.

INDEX

Publisher's Comment

Charles Patton is a history scholar of the finest tradition and has written an exciting, sometimes tear-wrenching account of the men who won this battle so important to the eventual expansion of our country. Andrew Jackson foresaw hundreds of thousands of pioneers settling along the Mississippi but never dreamed how *many* Americans would eventually call their homeland the territory that he and his brave men secured for our country. He saw the Louisiana Territory and later Texas as opening up doors all the way to the West and predicted our need for expansion to the Oregon Territory. He even warned of Cuba as a potential danger zone.

This book helps us understand the background in which the Battle of New Orleans was fought and how our country might have been vastly more limited had the battle not resulted in victory for the juvenile United States of America.

Jackson's most prized possession on this earth, aside from his devotion to the memory of his beloved Rachel, was the magnificent sword awarded him commemorating not just his, but *our* victory on the boggy grounds of Chalmette Plantation. Here against overwhelming odds, and facing brave and highly skilled British-Scotch-Irish forces, Jackson inspired camaraderie on the forefront of the battle, and led, by personal example, homespun wisdom and die-hard determination, this conglomerate of poorly equipped frontiersmen, militiamen, pirates, Creoles, Blacks, and loyal Indians, all fighting as a team for the new America, achieving what the British high command never dreamed possible, and repulsing the British from our shores, never to return again as our foes.

I am proud to say that Jackson entrusted to my great grandfather the sword which represented that battle and which, to Jackson, also represented the necessity to preserve our union. Though our country did subsequently endure the pangs of what seemed an inevitable Civil War, it has rebounded a strong nation based on high moral principles which we must never forget.

I am proud, as publisher of Charles Patton's book, to offer this story of courage and morality to our youth of today in hopes that examples can be found worthy of imitation, role models that have been sometimes difficult to find in our late 1900's leadership. I encourage other authors to bring alive our country's glorious past for our children to see. Let us help them get "high" from well-directed, raw courage and the success it brings rather than from drugs, satiated from the pure pleasure of a life of good works on this earth rather than from a life of sexual excess, and motivated not to seek money, power or fame nor to do just what is "popular" but to seek *"that one thing"* – that feeling of peace within one's heart, knowing that the life God gave has been well spent, when our "day is done."

Andrew Jackson Donelson, Jr. M.D.

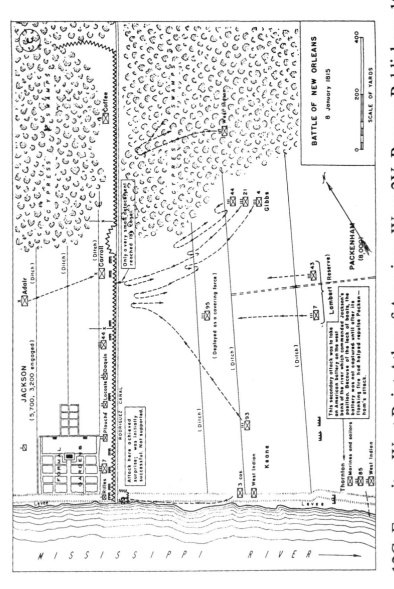

Map 12C, Esposito, West Point Atlas of American Wars 2V, Praeger Publishers, 1959.
Permission for use from Greenwood Publishing Group, Inc., Westport, Ct.